OUT OF THE GARDEN

Breaking Free From Sin and Shame

OUT OF THE GARDEN

Breaking Free From Sin and Shame

BY JEN HOFFMAN, LPC

Out of the Garden: Breaking Free From Sin and Shame
Copyright © 2023 by Jen Hoffman, All rights reserved

Requests for information should be addressed to: jenhoffmanlpc@gmail.com
www.jenhoffmanlpc.com

ISBN: 9798856890166

All rights reserved. No portion of this book may be reproduced, stored in a retrieval system, or transmitted in any form or by any means—electronic, mechanical, photocopy, recording, scanning, or other—except for brief quotations in critical reviews or articles, without the prior written permission of the publisher.

Independently published in Ohio

The ESV Global Study Bible®, ESV® Bible
Copyright © 2012 by Crossway.
All rights reserved.
Capitalization of pronouns incorporated by author

Scripture quotations marked (NIV) are taken from the Holy Bible, New International Version®, NIV®. Copyright © 1973, 1978, 1984, 2011 by Biblica, Inc. Used by permission of Zondervan. All rights reserved worldwide. www.zondervan.com The "NIV" and "New International Version" are trademarks registered in the United States Patent and Trademark Office by Biblica, Inc.
Capitalization of pronouns incorporated by author

Any resources cited (website, research, books, etc.) are offered for further review but not endorsed by the author.

The names and details of some individuals depicted here have been changed to protect anonymity.

Cover design: Jen Hoffman
Photoshoot font: Suby Studios

First printing September 2023 Printed in the United States of America

*I dedicate this book to my mom,
who taught me that true beauty is found
in a wise mind and calloused hands.
Thank you for your example of love and ministry.*

CONTENTS

A Quick Note	8	*A Quick Note*
Introduction	9	*Out of the Garden*
Chapter One	15	*Identity Crisis*
Chapter Two	27	*Consider the Source*
Chapter Three	38	*Abundant Life*
Chapter Four	46	*Intentional Rest*
Chapter Five	61	*Intentional Growth*
Chapter Six	76	*What's Holding You Back?*
Chapter Seven	94	*Transformed Mind*
Chapter Eight	105	*The Brain on Change*
Chapter Nine	114	*The Four C's*
Chapter Ten	128	*Women in the Word*
Chapter Eleven	136	*Two Worlds*
Chapter Twelve	142	*Take This Cup*
Conclusion	149	*The Story Continues*
Acknowledgement	151	
Notes	152	
About the Author	154	

A quick note…

Pssssst—before you get started—I want to say something. If you aren't sure what you think about the Bible, God, or all the things in between—this book is still for you. I poured my time into every word, doing my best not to be redundant or go on like a blathering fool. I have dreamed of writing a book for as long as I can remember, but the rose-colored glasses are off—this stuff is hard! I have to believe that if a bunch of yahoos had made up the Bible, they would have made the whole thing about their victories and not our need for a Savior. It's far too time-consuming to make up a storyline where you are always the sidekick.

Which brings me back to *this book*. I do mention the Bible *quite a bit*. I also mention some worldly influences because I'm not here for the Pharisees. I want to stand beside you, *in* and not *of* the world. I want this book to whittle away some of the resistance people feel toward God. I aim to offer Truth in a way that doesn't judge or discriminate. I hope you get a sense of that here. So if you are opening this book and thinking, *Jen—I don't want to go there*—I hear you. I really do. I also encourage you to read these pages as though you are investigating a case. With an inquiring mind that wants to know, determine if any evidence in your life supports this work to be true. While I am only human, still learning and growing, *God's Word is flawless and true.* And do you know what else? **It was meant for you.**

INTRODUCTION

Out of the Garden

I want more. It began as a whisper in my heart. I remember pushing it down, still reasonably aware of all we had been given. Adam squeezed my hand and looked knowingly into my eyes. "*Eve*," he would breathe out as his touch I would breathe in. Our thoughts were known to one another. We flowed as one stream, two rays of sunlight from the same ball of fire. He knew my heart and loved it as his own.

But that statement burned in me. I cupped fragrant flowers in my hands, looked into the eyes of the creatures, and somehow knew them too. The rhythm of the bubbling brooks matched my own heartbeat. We moved together in the Garden. *But there's more.* My eyes were drawn to the tree that day. Away from the form of my husband, away from our Creator walking through the Garden. What mystery was hidden in its fruit?

It all happened so quickly. One choice and then another. At that moment, we were stripped of His glory, clothed now in shame. I couldn't look our Creator in the eye. I hung my head low as He told us the consequences. I could hear the ache in His tone, the way His gentle kindness now moved toward discipline and pain. He was heartbroken. *What had we done?*

As we left the Garden, the clothing He had crafted felt itchy against my skin. Wearing the skin of animals we had once named and cared for was nauseating. The Tree of Life grew faint in the distance as I forever said goodbye to this perfect place.

Adam walked at a pace ahead of me, no longer at my side. I wondered if he would ever forgive me. I could no longer read the expression in his eyes or know his thoughts. A chasm was placed between us, and I knew then it was for always. Our feet fell hard against the jagged earth, and our eyes squinted against the night sky. For the first time, the hair on my arms raised, and I felt the chill of exposure in the night and the fear of uncertainty. Tears stung my eyes and stained my cheeks.

The full weight of the lie was settling in, and I could not turn back. The serpent had lied. *This was death.* Surely nothing could be worse than leaving our beautiful home and becoming strangers that labor and wander the earth.

Our Story Began in the Garden
When I consider the roots of our broken identity, I think it's important that we return to the Garden of Eden. Our desires were born there. We were designed to live where rivers meet land in a Garden that is no more. We were made to connect

with our Creator, oversee the good of the earth, and develop disentangled relationships. In writing this fictional account of Adam and Eve, my heart ached for what was lost. Man's outcome changed at the Tree, but our intended design did not. While He may have been dismayed, God was not surprised in the Garden of Eden. I don't want to spoil the ending, but He knew what would happen and had a plan.

God wrote our story, wanting us to know our immense worth through Him. It was always meant to be a relationship, a love story. He designed us with the freedom to choose, but He never intended for us to experience the agony and separation of sin. When sin entered the world, it carried with it the lie that free will in a relationship with God would not be enough. Sin created confusion and questions about God's character. It separated us from God and caused natural consequences.

Genesis three recorded the Fall of man as Eve was deceived by the serpent (Genesis 3:1-6). In this account, we observe Adam and Eve's immediate response to sin, God's questions for them, and the consequences that followed. We return to the Garden to understand the ramifications that continue to exist in our world today. It is the cautionary tale of an entire storyline changing—*just like that.*

Our Connection to God
Sin's presence complicated our rapport with God. We are told that Adam and Eve saw that they were naked and hid from the Lord (Gen. 3:7, 8). They were not surprised by God's presence but rather had grown accustomed to walking with Him. His presence was the norm—their sin was not. Genesis 3:12-14 shows us that God asked Adam and Eve why they disobeyed

Him. He already knew the answer, but I imagine He wanted them to speak for themselves. Communication and accountability were fundamental as they faced their Creator. Adam quickly blamed Eve (Gen. 3:12), and she blamed the serpent (Gen. 3:13). God did not question the serpent because He no doubt had little time or patience for the Father of Lies. Instead, He cursed the serpent and noted that he would one day be crushed by the woman's offspring (Gen. 3:14, 15). Jesus would later fulfill that promise, offering redemption and breaking sin's hold. God extended grace and healing before stating the consequences.

Our Bodies
Our distorted view of our bodies began with the onset of sin. We do not wear the proud skin of image-bearers but instead, find fault with our earthly forms. We experience shame, disappointment, and longing for something else. Adam and Eve were instantly aware of their nudity, which was a new concept for them. It was as though their minds were unlocked, allowing influence outside of God's protection to bustle through the doors. Our enemy presented sin quietly and divisively. It was never intended for mankind to bear the burden of humiliation and shame. This exposure was both physical and spiritual in nature.

Second Corinthians 5:2,3 (NIV) says, "Meanwhile we groan, longing to be clothed instead with our heavenly dwelling, because when we are clothed, we will not be found naked." Adam and Eve were not only aware of their nakedness but the reality that they had been stripped of God's glory and presence. While our dissatisfaction with our bodies began in the Garden, it continues to be a stronghold in our world today. We struggle with our weight and appearance, but we long for the weight of His glory.

We've felt the pain of being naked, of longing to be clothed. We've been stripped of love in our relationships. We've been stripped of pregnancy, children we don't know, and bodies that might not cooperate. We've been stripped of life, watching people we love fight to live and lose that battle. We've been stripped of comfort, dignity, safety, wants, and needs. We, too, have felt exposed.

Our Relationships
Sin has damaged the bonds between family members since the beginning of time. Genesis 3:16 warns that childbirth will be painful and laborious. I believe this pain extends to the challenging relationships between siblings, the anguish of losing a child, and the hardship of longing for children. We've eagerly waited to conceive—or conceived before we were ready for that decision. We've faced complications during pregnancy, the worry that stillness brings, and the discomfort of a swift kick to the ribs. We've mourned over the lives that didn't join us--or those that did for too short of a time. Even as I write this, I think of our pregnancies and those lives I don't know. The Fall has made tombs of our bodies.

Sin severed the marriage union, creating unquenchable desire and barriers to communication. Genesis 3:16 (NIV) says, "Your desire will be for your husband, and he will rule over you." The Garden marriage balanced love and respect with clearly defined roles and boundaries. Unfortunately, sin has brought about confusion regarding our original design. This troubling dynamic has led to abuse, neglect, and mismanaged households since the beginning of time. In Genesis 3:23, God banished them from the Garden, which was immediately guarded by armed cherubim. *Heavily guarded, in fact.* These cherubim had flaming swords, sending a clear message that the couple was no longer welcome or trusted in this place. The path was broken.

Our Hope
Even still, our hope is not lost. God's response to sin reveals that He values honest communication, personal responsibility, and justice. God fashioned clothing out of animals He'd created with care in order to protect Adam and Eve from the elements and the shame of their naked bodies (Gen. 3:21). This symbolized the many sacrifices that would follow. This imagery is powerful because His first reckoning for sin foreshadowed what would ultimately be His last.

Where are these whispers of wanting more in your life? Maybe you've felt stuck while watching others move forward. You've observed job opportunities, successful relationships, financial freedom, personal fitness, and beauty. They sparkle, they glow, and they make it look so easy. You see satisfaction, purpose, and meaning. A quiet whisper inside your heart says, "I want more." *I believe you were made to have it.*

1

Identity Crisis

What do you want to be known for? Ask yourself this question as you read these chapters. It's the question that lives deep inside each of us, whether or not we know it by name. We measure our worth by how well we can answer this question. Our identity is shaped by how we share ourselves with the world, usually through the resources we've been given. We present ourselves through social media, work, relationships, and how we spend our time, money, and resources. We each have a picture of the person we want the world to see. What does yours look like?

I can tell you that the picture I hold near and dear to my heart is that of a woman who can do it all. Given the same 24 hours as the rest of humanity, I'm trying to follow Jesus, connect with my husband and kids, thrive in my relationships, have a clean(ish) home, and provide healthy, home-cooked meals.

Fine, yes, I will make them myself. The food is meant to nourish and be enjoyed, not pushed around the plate, and later replaced by cheese crackers and pretzels. I would like to have game nights without arguing, complaint-free vacations, and photographic evidence that we smiled occasionally. Let's go for gold and add healthy future relationships with my kids, joyful years of retirement with my husband, and grandchildren that magnify their parents' most *gregarious* qualities. I'd like them to receive what they've given tenfold, please.

I consider all of this while balancing the time I spend with or without people I love—while also remaining open to new friendships. Open, minus the risk of taking on too many while not seeming closed off. I juggle these ways of relating to others while deciding whether to be a farmer, counselor, artist, or writer. I've decided I want all of the above, and they will have to take turns in due season. If my calculations are correct, I'll need to give up sleep.

I have held onto these dreams while navigating marriage and stay-at-home motherhood. Those early years are a blur to me now, but at the time, they were all-consuming. Wanting to be chosen—and then chosen again every day. Waiting to say "I do" and feeling frightened by the moments I find that "I don't." Working so hard to reduce two into one, only to hope that one day that number would multiply again. Hours and months of waiting for life. Preparing for birth with little to no knowledge of how or when it would occur. The minutes and days of adjusting, healing, and blending together as a family. Letting go of what life looked like before children, the babies that didn't join us, and my expectations when our first child finally arrived. With time, I let go of their little hands as they need me less. *Did I hold them enough? Where did the time go?* Quick, quick, slow. Just as I learned the routine, the steps would change.

I entered this sacred pact of women with unclear lines between my childhood experiences and my view of our growing family. Some patterns felt inevitable, making it strenuous to hope for anything else. I had difficulty knowing which hopes were realistic and which cycles were unavoidable. Some chains appeared unbreakable. Some habits formed so naturally. I lived in the tension between healing and growing. Holding on and letting go. My identity changed many times throughout the process. Motherhood has exposed the deepest roots of exile and has produced the sweetest fruits of freedom.

Identity
How has your identity changed? How would you describe yourself, now that you've lived through a bit of love and marriage, in a full or empty nest, and you have experienced life and loss? I imagine you have some of the same tension in your own story. You are balancing the demands with the desire to shape a life that you love. Your attention is divided, no doubt. In love, it is constantly changing, even when you've known someone for the longest time. There are days I think I have my husband completely figured out—and then he surprises me. If you are a parent, you are adapting to the ever-changing roles that each milestone presents. I know many people who have questions about their identity as their children have grown older.

My motivation to answer this question of worth and identity began a few years ago. I was thinking about what it meant to find our identity in Christ. *What on earth does that mean, exactly?* While I identify as a Christ follower, my choices don't always reflect that. I have often limited God's Truth to being skin deep. It's easy to feel like an imposter when I see the space between who God says I am and who I see in the mirror. What caused me to move from the depth of Christ's comfort to being disengaged? I wanted to find the missing piece between consistency in my faith and my unbound, wandering heart.

I quickly found that my inconsistencies were linked to the way I think. More often than not, I put limitations on what I believe God can do with my life. I worry that His grace has run out on my exhausting and continual relationship with sin. I feel as though *this time,* He has had enough. I wrestle with doing too many things at once. This may surprise you (given the earlier description of how I spend my time), but I squeeze as much out of a day as possible. I do this because, at my core, I believe there will not be enough time. I worry about what I will be known for and what I will have to show for the time I've been given. I want to finish well.

When I had the opportunity to speak at a mom's camp, I knew this was the content. I had engaged with so many women in different life stages, wrestling with their identities. I noticed a theme as women's confidence was distorted by the demand to appear a certain way. So many of my friends and women I know wear this banner that says, "I'm not enough." It scrolls across their lives while, at the same time, they are moving in four different directions with barely a moment in between. They—and really, I mean we—walk the tightrope between longing and settling. There's not enough time in the day, so we make sacrifices. We keep it to ourselves, fearing that our thoughts would scare others away. That causes us to feel a myriad of things, depending on what these sacrifices have meant to us. Like moss, bitterness and disappointment grow in the darkest, hardest places.

Materialism

My husband and I have a running joke that when I go shopping, I make a "store visit" to assess productivity, check out the products, make suggestions, etc. I say it with a sigh, as though I'm preparing to clock in for the day. If I come home with several bags (which is *only sometimes*), I shake my head as I tell him they desperately need me to review some products. The whole thing just cracks me up. We both know I'm an avid shopper, and *Mama needs her fix.*

I know how it must sound. I want to tell you that I'm a bargain shopper, and they honestly were great deals. *Most of them, anyway.* But at the core, I battle with an element of materialism. I'm not putting my hope in these things, but I am putting them in my home. I will wear the clothes, use the gadgets, and believe in the promise that they will add to my life in some way. I will fill online carts and place hearts beside future purchases. I create categorized boards with thousands of ideas to update and upgrade our home.

I'm not suggesting that we stop buying things. We are human; sometimes we need things. However, this is an area where we compare ourselves to others—our homes, wardrobes, occupations, vehicles, favorite pastimes, etc. If we aim to keep up with the Joneses, we will likely overextend ourselves and attach value to our purchases. We are no longer attempting to simplify or add to our lives—we are trying to add up.

Body Image

Modern technology has altered our standards of beauty. We have access to advanced photography tools, reconstructing filters, high-quality makeup, and social media to share it instantly. Beauty treatments are available at a higher cost, attempting to reverse the aging process and slow down the signs of time. We can be tucked, lifted, smoothed out, and made pretty. We make time to work out because, let's face it, we are no longer hunters and gatherers. Movement has been segregated from our schedule and considered a luxury, rather than a necessity. We have numerous ways to modify our eating habits. Eat more—or less—to look a certain way. "*Anything can be fixed*," we are subtly told. Our unique qualities and asymmetries suddenly become flaws in need of repair.

We face an epidemic of distorted views about our bodies and health. We can scroll through stories of massive weight loss and see pictures of what someone ate today. Our eyes believe what they see, even if the person is nipped, tucked, or sucking in. The overarching theme is that anyone can be skinny if they try hard enough. This is simply not true.

In middle school, we learned about body types—endomorphs, mesomorphs, and ectomorphs. We learned that the ectomorph, a lean body type with difficulty gaining weight, makes up 3% of our population.[1] That number was fascinating and relatively low. The teacher informed us that these types are part of our genetic makeup and cannot be changed over time. While diet and exercise are factors, the structure and tendencies of the body remain the same. I played soccer then and knew by my toned quads that I was a solid mesomorph. I also felt relieved knowing that no amount of starving myself or working out would change my appearance. This lesson was an influential building block in accepting my design. This lesson is lost in modern media.

Every body type has its hang-ups. Even with the body-positive movement, shame and social discomfort still surround our weight. I've caught myself telling others about the next plan I'll start or how much I've enjoyed working out. The sub-text reads, "Don't judge me. I am trying." Our bodies are the least interesting thing about us, but social media makes them appear as the most important thing we have to offer.

I'm not skinny enough. I'm not pretty enough. I'm not a good mom. I'm not a good friend. I'm not a good enough wife. I wish I was more successful. I don't think I can be independent. I'm not attractive enough. I need to do more. I need to be better. These thoughts are sneaky. They creep in quietly and settle quickly. Before you know it, they are moving about freely in your mind, taking up space and using all the hot water. They work their way into conversations and cause you to question yourself.

These lies on our hearts cause us to view our humanity as a deficit that makes us less presentable to others. Some views have been passed down by previous generations, and others we've picked up along the way. We bear the weight of these labels in our relationships. It's a heavy burden if and when we discover that we do not "live up to" someone else's expectations. The people around us sometimes project their ideas onto our lives. They might lack the confidence to be in their skin, and suddenly we are not okay, either. It almost validates the lies we believe. An untamed mind will quickly say, *See? I knew others could see it. I'm not enough.* We trudge along with the idea that we will never be enough if we don't have *more.*

Scarcity Thinking

This is called scarcity thinking. It is the mindset that we require more resources, time, relationships, and opportunities to feel satisfied. It's the difference between a growth and a fixed mindset. Scarcity thinking causes us to believe that another person's success could interfere with our own. One person's gain could be our loss. It is in our nature to compare, and we are conditioned to compete. Women are often pitted against each other to fill limited positions. Our culture is set up to make us feel as though we have fallen behind.

Worchel, Lee, and Adewole introduced scarcity as a concept in their 1975 study. These researchers hypothesized that we "value things more when they're in limited supply."[2] Study participants observed cookie jars that had an abundance of cookies or were scarce. They also believed that more people would be participating in the study, which created an inner struggle with competition and demand. The results suggested that participants preferred jars with one or two cookies to those that were full. They appeared more desirable.

The scarcity principle became a standard economic marketing principle. Companies limited their quantity to make products appear more valuable, used time to pressure a quick decision, and only allowed certain people to access the items. An empty shelf continues to signal our minds today as we want to be included, feel important, and not feel as though we're missing out.

Proverbs 23:7 tells us that our minds believe what we tell them. You are what you think. If you think you can't—then you most likely won't. However, hope can soar with the simple utterance of the word *believe*. I imagine Ted Lasso and his handwritten yellow sign taped to the locker room wall. He said to believe, and it brought people together.[3] Perception is everything.

Scarcity thinking is a self-fulfilling prophecy. Our lives become small when we focus on what we do not have. This can have positive outcomes, but it depends on what we seek. According to Sendhil Mullainathan and Eldar Shafir, Ph.D., in their book *Scarcity: The New Science of Having Less and How it Defines Our Lives,* "When scarcity captures the mind, it focuses our attention on using what we have most effectively."[4]

Scarcity thinking can go either way—it can eliminate distractions or prevent us from nurturing other necessary aspects of our lives. The outcome depends on what we value and the sacrifices we will make. It all comes down to what our minds believe is missing. Shafir, Ph.D., and Mullainathan's research showed that a scarcity mindset often leads to the following potentially adverse outcomes:

- Trade-off thinking (either/or)
- Lacking impulse control
- Rigid thinking
- Tunnel vision (only focused on this one thing)
- Neglecting important tasks (in place of urgent ones)
- Lowers IQ, which can lead to average or deficient functioning

A scarcity mindset demands our attention and causes us to alter the way we make decisions. Oftentimes, it reveals our idols. In the absence of wants or needs, we often seek to find comfort in time, resources, and relationships rather than relying on God.

A scarcity mindset presents itself as early as preschool—the game "musical chairs" tells us there are not enough seats at the table. It shows up in small ways: *Is there space for me? Do they want me to join?* It becomes apparent in significant ways: *Will I be able to provide for my family? Am I enough? Am I too much?* It shows up often: *Why do I care about this? What's wrong with me that I can't get past this?*

Danger or difficult circumstances cause us to feel as though there is not enough protection around us. We may have received a clear message in the past that our sense of safety could be taken away from us in an instant. Vulnerability is more about feeling unguarded rather than deeply known. It feels more like a place of weakness than a safe connection.

A mind preoccupied by what is lacking is far from peaceful. It is actively angling, always considering how to get ahead. Colossians 3:15 (NIV) says, "Let the peace of Christ rule in your hearts, since as members of one body you were called to peace. And be thankful." A mind ruled by peace can rest in gratitude. A mind governed by *more* cannot rest.

I imagine us using a measuring stick to determine our worth. In medieval times, tally sticks were used to record a debt. According to David Graeber, author of *Debt: The First 5,000 Years,* "Tally sticks were quite explicitly IOUs: both parties to a transaction would take a hazelwood twig, notch it to indicate the amount owed, and then split it in half. The creditor would keep one half, called "the stock" (hence the origin of the term "stock holder") and the debtor kept the other, called "the stub" (hence the origin of the term "ticket stub.)"[5] The rough edges matched one another, tracing the debtor back to the one that was owed. In China, during the Han Dynasty, the stick was broken after the debt was settled *(Author's note: I learned about this system long after writing this chapter, but I am blown away by how it fits the following analogy. God is so good at tying it all together!)*

We often measure our worth by what the people around us are doing. I imagine Jesus holding the stick and asking us to consider our motivation. The world tells us we'll love our lives when we measure up. Religion tells us we'll be saved by the measure of our works. Social media says you'll feel better when your measurement is less. The woke movement tells us to measure our actions by other people's reactions. We are socially, emotionally, physically, and spiritually in debt.

We measure our bodies, husbands, kids, homes, work, and worth, and I imagine Jesus breaking the stick, quickly crafting a rugged cross. He says *"STOP!* Stop measuring yourself by what the world is telling you. Let Me be the measure of your infinite worth." *He took both halves.* He removed our debt. Jesus multiplied our value by infinity. He offered a way out of daily comparisons and temporary worth.

Take it to Heart

- Our identity is often shaped by the way others see us. How would people describe you based on your social media, what you talk about, and how you spend your time?

- Who/what are your most significant influences?

- What are ways you compare yourself to others?

- Where have you experienced scarcity thinking in your life?

- How does this influence the way you view yourself?

Take it to God

- Read Psalm 139:23, 24 — offer this as a prayer to God.

- Is there anything in your life that has been overlooked as a result of the influence in your life?

2

Consider the Source

Have I told you about the time we had a stalker? This little family of mine and I were singing with the windows down as we rolled up to our friend's vacation home. We were staying with him after a recent divorce from a toxic marriage. We pulled in to find the two arguing in the driveway, his former partner swaying on too high of heels as she screamed closely into his face. We rolled up the windows as she spotted us and briskly approached the vehicle. I was so focused on letting my kids know they were safe that I did not hear what was said. When my husband returned to the car, his face was pale, and his innocence was compromised. Her verbal assault included graphic sexual details about our friend and this woman that my husband still has not repeated to me *to this day*.

 Once she was gone, we settled into the house and did our best to move on. Our friend is a cup-half-full kind of guy, even as water spews out of the cracks and begs for repair. While changing into our swimsuits, the outside door to our guest room rattled. When I called out to my husband and our friend, they were both in the house, along with the kids. I went outside to find our rental car with every door open as though she had rifled through it. *She was relentless.* Not only had she tried to break in, but she waited for us to return home from dinner that evening. With an intimidating pause, she finally rolled out. I couldn't see her glare over the headlight, but my cheeks grew hot as I watched her drive away. Needless to say, I didn't sleep.

We moved on. I'm not one to sweep things under the rug, but our friend wanted that. I become clumsy when uneasy, as though I'm tripping over the issues underfoot. In the following days, I drowned my phone, broke my husband's phone, and nearly broke my DSLR lens. My husband tried to be understanding, but he grew increasingly less patient as I continued down my destructive path. We argued quietly behind closed doors, the dreadful insecurities of what would come next never spoken aloud. The bizarre trip continued with other circumstances that are not worth mentioning. I felt trapped in this odd little bubble and without my phone, I couldn't reach the outside world.

I felt like I was drowning. I prayed to God and said just that. He felt so distant at that moment, as though *even He* could not bear to be around me. I begged him to give me some sense of peace because I feared I would continue to wreak havoc and have more conflict in my clumsiness. *I held my breath underwater and felt consumed.*

While we were there, I was listening to an album by one of my favorite bands. I found and played one song non-stop (on my husband's phone since mine had perished in the water), and its words became my mantra. It described being pulled under, with sound effects meant to mimic a storm in the distance. It's hard to describe, but it sounded like a sinking ship. I closed my eyes and envisioned the hull bulging and creaking under the pressure of water.

As a child, I daydreamed about being a mermaid and exploring sunken treasure ships, a part of the world no one could reach. *Didn't we all?* This song brought on less of a daydream and more of a daymare. I could see myself sinking with the ship, my eyes closed, and my will resigned. I was not seeking escape or for my life to be over. This wasn't about wanting it *all* to end. I did welcome any sense of numbness that might short-circuit the electrifying feeling of being raw nerves and loose wires. I sought peace and quiet.

At some point, finally lucid and no longer clumsy, I paid attention to the words. Just about every song on the album was about drowning—*lost, tumbling down, drowning, smothering, buried, swallowed, sinking.*[6] I felt like I was awake. Like a splash of water to the face, each lyric hit me. How could an ounce of hope sink in when I filled my mind with these lies?

I was the one telling myself I was drowning. Technically the music suggested the idea and I drank the juice. No wonder I felt hopeless! I couldn't escape the idea that I was drowning because I repeatedly and melodically pumped these words into my brain. I could not tell the difference between being consumed by my problems and my problems being consumed by God's grace. I longed for rest and relief.

I share this story because I want to reiterate that the things we tell ourselves are important. Our thoughts shape our lives. I can live in Truth and follow Jesus wholeheartedly and *still* have moments where I believe I'm unlovable. Unsavable. Unchanged. Unredeemed. While I have faced more significant challenges, this experience caused me to question my value and identity.

Our walk with Jesus is not linear. This is the reminder I needed to restore my view of my identity. We do not take two steps forward and three steps back, although it does feel that way. We conquer peaks and valleys, moving forward and carrying wisdom and grace. While each additional valley may feel like defeat, we do not have to claw our way out alone. It feels as though we've gone from a restored creation to someone of little value in no time at all. In my case, I needed to consider the source of these lies that were rooted in my heart and mind.

Where have you felt these lies in *your* heart? Where have you felt consumed? As you go through the chapters ahead, those are the questions I want you to ask yourself. Your story is likely different from mine, but I imagine you have experienced complicated relationships with uncontrollable circumstances that have left you feeling disheveled. How has that impacted who you believe you are?

The pain in our lives also makes it difficult to be present and reflective. Our minds are full of dangerous thoughts. We turn the background noise up to eleven in order to drown out the worry or fear. Anxiety and depression are at an all-time high since the pandemic. It seems as if all of the trouble tucked away in our minds began to overflow as a result of this frightening time. Out poured the issues that could no longer be stuffed inside. We faced a scarcity of safety that left us feeling raw, exposed, and unsure of one another.

Our Emotions
We experience a range of emotions throughout our lifetime. Many are positive and make life interesting—joy, excitement, satisfaction, love. They add meaning. We are connected through positive experiences. When we are experiencing positive emotions, we are more likely to feel energized, confident, and ready to connect with others. When we are struggling emotionally, we feel their absence.

Our out-of-balance emotions are an indicator that we need rest. When we become overwhelmed by anxiety, depression, or something in between, our body demands a moment to stop and consider what is happening. It all feels like too much. We often become dysregulated, which means we cannot process our emotions effectively. At the same time, we feel pressure to keep moving.

Emotions stem from a number of things. We may have unmet needs from childhood that become expectations in adult relationships. We may be caught off by pain in the present as it springs up out of nowhere. We experience feelings that influence the course of our day. They are an expression of our inner sense of worth and our relational needs.

Marriage reflects these places most acutely. We commit ourselves, flaws and all, to be vulnerable and dependent on this other flawed person. We wound each other. We are two separate minds working toward one goal. *What is that goal exactly?* It's not always clear, is it? We have separate expectations about what marriage even means. We continue because the love we have outweighs the challenges we face. I consider my husband to be my best friend, but that does not prevent us from experiencing confusion and hurt in our marriage.

In a way, our families recreate patterns we experienced during our developmental years. When our marriages or children experience a milestone that was significant in our development, it might spark some old feelings. For example, if someone had a painful or traumatic experience at a certain age, she might begin to feel unsettled as her own child reaches that age. This is not conscious or intentional—it is instinctual.

In many ways, we need to challenge our negative ideas about thoughts and emotions. Jeremiah 17:9 (ESV) tells us, "The heart is deceitful above all things, and desperately sick; who can understand it?" Our untrustworthy, sickly hearts get a bad rep. Most of us have had dark thoughts, confusing feelings, and at least one weird dream that would make us blush if anyone could read our minds. It's no wonder we tuck our twisted little minds away while giving them the side eye.

Negative beliefs about our emotionality have also created confusion in the church, as people often dismiss *all* feelings as problematic. Some believe that depression and anxiety are the result of weak faith or loose morals. Pew dwellers sharply suggest that if someone sinned less, they wouldn't be experiencing these symptoms. I recall reading advice for a woman who was deeply depressed. "Go bake cookies for others," she was advised. Poof! Her depression was healed. I snapped that book shut and stuffed it away. As an advocate for mental health, I find responses like those listed above to be offensive and critical of an already hurting world.

While we may not rely on our feelings to guide our decisions, they are an essential part of our design. Our thoughts and emotions are often powerful communicators of our internal life. They exist for a reason. Some feelings are uncomfortable. We say, "I'm fine," which really means I have feelings I need to express.

We can extend grace and be gentle toward this part of ourselves. Just as we approached our sin with curiosity, we remain open to what our emotions are telling us. This does not suggest that we allow them to direct our path. By seeking wisdom, we are removing the power they hold over us and submitting them to God. Transformation occurs when we are obedient to God and willing to search our hearts to understand what separates us from His peace.

Grief Requires Rest
In times of grief and loss, our need for rest is even greater. I have observed the grief process with clients, which is painful and consuming, like a wound that won't heal. It slows people down and wears them out. It is completely exhausting. Many people describe grief as an empty space they carry with them. The emphasis is on who or what is missing, making it difficult

to think about anything else. They experience shame, regret, and often guilt for moving forward.

Often the grieving have sought counseling because they need a place to talk about who or what was lost. At the same time, they want to move on and find a new sense of normalcy. They want to remember and forget all at once. Their pain calls them to slow down, to take on less, and to walk slowly through this loss.

When I picture the grief described by others, I imagine a human heart with a hole in it, pumping laboriously along. The sense of emptiness stops people in their tracks. Feelings about their loss arise out of nowhere, making it difficult to complete daily tasks. This produces anxiety because they cannot predict the next time they will feel this way.

A grieving person often feels like a burden to others who have not experienced the same loss. Our culture promotes moving on quickly, suggesting that emotional expression or feeling stuck shows weakness. Finding people who understand is difficult, so the world is reduced to a smaller circle. Grief is a lonely path when someone lacks a proven support system. The wound remains open, a black hole pulling people inward.

We Can Allow Grief to Transform Us
Grief is messy. Engaging with it requires us to get our hands dirty, so to speak. I envision the black hole becoming fertile soil. Like a tiny seed, we bury the loss for growth, not removal. We cover it there, knowing it will transform undercover and out of sight. The source will die away before it can yield new life. We acknowledge that something is lost or broken down. It

makes no sense to the naked eye, but we trust the process. Burying the seed represents letting go of the way things appeared, the life we envisioned, and our plans. Letting go is not the same as forgetting. It is a choice to heal and move on, allowing the growth of something new. Acceptance is an important step in the grief process because it provides freedom.

What if we decide to cast the seeds away and see what grows? *I don't want to think about this. I can't do this.* It has been my experience that weeds are happy to grow in the place of more desirable choices. Choosing to ignore our pain does not make it go away. It causes it to take some other form. It's hurting, too, you know. It's as though it requires a disguise in order to sneak out undetected.

We select seeds with intentionality, knowing that we will reap what we sow. Evidence of new life appears with the first sign of a sprout. We can allow the hurt to blossom into a genuine life that knows suffering and moving forward. We may always miss what was lost, but we are still here. We are still growing and healing. Figure 1 is an illustration of how grief feels vs. how we can grow from it.

Growth occurs when we address our pain and allow ourselves to express our emotions outwardly. Like the buried seed, our thoughts and beliefs about the loss will influence what grows in us. Anxiety weakens when we find healthy outlets. We no longer hold in our feelings or allow them to explode out of us at inopportune times. Healthy grief moves with a person, not through them. It becomes a part of the story, not the whole story or its ending. Your identity may be shaped by loss, but not defined by it.

Grief counseling holds a special place in my heart because it offers space for people to share their love for someone who is no longer with them. Clients can say a name that has often been banished or discouraged in their own world because it is too painful to utter. It can be a place for people to share stories of someone they loved without feeling like a burden to anyone else. I feel honored to walk through it with them and humbled by their brave vulnerability.

Jesus modeled healthy emotional expression in His ministry. He expressed sadness with tears, disappointment with direct and appropriate confrontation, and righteous anger with correction. Jesus demonstrated that there is a time and a place for us to let it all out. We've been given a range of responses. With a little fine-tuning, we can use them to express ourselves productively.

Figure 1

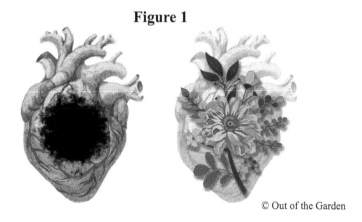

© Out of the Garden

Take it to Heart

- What triggers let you know when you feel overwhelmed or need rest?

- What do you believe to be true about our thoughts and emotions? What messages have you received from your family, friends, and church?

- What new information has this chapter provided to shape your view of emotional expression?

Take it to God

- Read Psalm 69. Can you relate to David feeling as though He was drowning? What verse offers hope to you?

- If it came up for you, lift up the places you have experienced disappointment in the absence of provision or protection.

- Can you see how God has brought you to where you are today through your circumstances? Make the connection and thank Him for the goodness you can find.

3

Abundant Life

We are in summer now, and some days pass quickly. I feel like I'm holding a press conference as I answer questions about what we'll do, who we'll see, and when the kids can have screen time. I am the gatekeeper. *I want more peace.* I wrestle with wanting more time for myself, feeling selfish when the thought crosses my mind. Balancing the quality of our time with the quantity of conflict is exhausting. I would much rather be a cheerleader than a referee, but this is the season we are in.

Parenting today feels like a battle to protect childhood. I want my kids to be fancy-free and footloose—not to become hunchbacks that require special-order glasses from all the years of staring at a tiny, glowing screen. We create boundaries, talk about safety, and monitor relationships. *I want more understanding as we do our best to protect them.*

The pace of our lives makes it difficult to rest. Slowing down sounds lovely, but it is not always possible. The increasing demand from sports and social outlets leaves little time to think, let alone sleep. *I remember sleep. It was my favorite.* Even in summer, our days are filled with demands.

My favorite moments are when we go outside and do something *just because*. It seems odd to be so filled by the mundane moments, and yet they are like an oasis for my thirsty soul. The kids will run through the yard to catch fireflies as we sit on the porch nearby. The dogs chase each other while the cats pounce out of the bushes. We are serenaded by a symphony of crickets and bullfrogs. It reminds me that we moved here to slow down and enjoy wide-open spaces.

I have nothing to prove in the still, quiet moments. The warm sun that soothes my skin is followed by the crisp night air that refreshes me. God's creation is a love letter that invites us to know Him and fall into step with Him. Leaves fall like confetti as though they are a celebration of new life. The veins on the leaves match those that carry blood through our bodies, reminding us of His consistency in providing signs of life. The rhythmic cadence of nature helps me to relax. While these moments allow me to connect with His creation, intentional rest offers space to relate to His design *for me*.

The Abundant Life
If scarcity thinking drives us to believe that we'll never measure up, an abundance mindset allows us to let go and rest in immeasurable grace. This grace is found in a relationship with Christ that is based on faith and surrender. As it turns out, I cannot manipulate or curate my identity in Christ to make it

more aesthetically pleasing. The abundant life I seek is found in my genuine connection with Him. His influence naturally moves me. His ways become my ways. My skin-deep faith is enriched simply by loving Him. He alone can soften my hardened artery walls.

An abundant life begins in the mind. What is your definition of abundance? The world's definition of an abundance mindset includes pursuing the "good life" that is protected by monetary freedom. There are books lining shelves that promise an abundance of beauty, wealth, and success. We associate the word with *more* and picture material evidence of having it all. Social media confirms that we will feel fulfilled when the ache for *more* subsides within us. We strive, struggle, and sweat—never entirely losing that hunger.

Whatever version of abundance I have tucked away in my heart will divulge my motives and biases. That version is always most apparent when I feel stressed, overwhelmed, or burdened by my circumstances. I'm trying to balance my wants with others' needs, and the strain is rudely revealing. When there is not enough of me to go around, the frustration shows whatever core idea pushes me to my limits.

In contrast, when I read the Bible as the solution to the scarcity problem, it becomes a retaining wall to my otherwise eroding resolve. Once I prioritize finding a quiet space between the distractions and the demands, Scripture fills me in a refreshing way. I find stories of courage, unbelievable circumstances, and dramatic historical perspectives. It is filled with love and hate, life and death. David pours out his heart in the Psalms—even suggesting what God could do to his enemies. *I didn't know we could do that.* The Song of Solomon gets spicy and reminds us that God designed sex to be desired and enjoyed. Solomon had many wives, *and with lines like his, I can see why.* I'm kidding, of course. *I only have eyes for one man.* This couple's anticipation is a gripping reminder of the beauty that lies in the waiting and wanting. The Bible reframes the places where soul meets body, offering grace and understanding.

The Word Came to Life

Reading the Bible to intentionally become more like Jesus illuminates my blind spots, which include sin I have renamed and filed away as *not that bad* or *this doesn't hurt anyone.* Hebrews 4:12 (ESV) tells us," For the word of God is living and active, sharper than any two-edged sword, piercing to the division of soul and of spirit, of joints and of marrow, and discerning the thoughts and intentions of the heart." I love the imagery in this verse as it describes God's Truth reaching the parts of us that are so deep within, even we don't know them. He knows the places that go beyond the microscope into each woven fiber of my being. I am changed on a cellular level when I allow His Truth to sink beneath the skin and permeate my muscles. It pours into the very marrow of who I am. Every crack and crevice is reclaimed, swelling with life and creative ideas. This happens when I separate my worth from the world.

Restored Identity

Our identity is restored through our relationship with Christ. We are offered freedom. The Old Testament is filled with promises that we would be rescued—the New Testament is evidence that God meant what He said. In a way, the abundance mindset offers monetary freedom, as well. As scarcity reveals our idols, abundance releases us from them.

Jesus is fondly remembered and revered. While most of His ministry took place in three years, He changed lives forever. He gave us an escape from sin and our broken past. For every lie that says we are unredeemable, there is a verse that reminds us we are unbound, unchained, and free indeed. Some attributes of this freedom are shared in the verses below:

Our Relationship With God
- We can ask for help (Ps. 118:5)
- We are set free by Truth (John 8:32)
- Our debt is paid (Rom. 13:8)
- We are equipped to serve others (Rom. 13:8, Gal. 5:13, 1 Pet. 2:16, 17, 1 Cor. 9:19)

Our New Identity
- Our slave identity is removed (Gal. 5:1, Rom. 6:14, 18, 22, Rom. 8:2)
- We are God's handiwork (Eph. 2:10)
- We were fearfully and wonderfully made (Ps.139:14)
- We bear His image (Gen. 1:27)
- We are His adopted children (Eph. 1:5)
- We are made royal (1 Pet. 2:9) and new (2 Cor. 5:17)

We are so much more than we live out in our daily lives.

Free Will Vs. Freedom
Our world muddies the water between free will and freedom. God gave us free will to make choices. A free will directs us toward things that will make us happy or feel good. It is our nature to make choices based on what we want. In 1 Corinthians 10:23, Paul tells us that while all things are permitted, they may not be the best thing for us. He calls us

away from the culture that tells us we can do what we want and points us to make decisions with accountability.

We live out our freedom when we express gratitude for our ransom. We recognize the cost. We value independence in our country and celebrate it by honoring the lives that were sacrificed on our behalf. A grateful heart perceives boundaries as protectors, not barriers. Just as a fire is safest in a fireplace, some limits protect us from harm. Can you imagine arguing that fire should be able to go wherever it wants? In the same way, we honor Christ by living with accountability, boundaries, and faith. Freedom in Christ offers protection from choices that could harm us.

Put it to the Test
Sometimes it is difficult to differentiate between scarcity and abundance thinking. Something can seem like a good or right choice, but it does not fit in our life, at least in this season. I battle my inner people pleaser that suggests I'm hurting someone's feelings or letting them down. Even with careful consideration, we may not be able to discern why something is sticking like a square peg in a round hole. Am I facing a closed door, or am I intentionally being stretched and reshaped?

In John 10:1-16, Jesus tells the parable of sheep that respond to the shepherd's voice. They do not go to strangers, but they will recognize the voice of their master. In verse 10 (ESV), He said, "The thief comes only to steal and kill and destroy. I came that they may have life and have it abundantly." When we become familiar with God's Truth, we can distinguish between what He is telling us and lies that are only meant to deceive and distract us. The consistency and simplicity of God's Word allow us to rest in Him. If the thing I seek will steal my mind, kill my joy, or destroy my relationships, it is not from God. I want to seek the things that will enhance my faith, my time with loved ones, and my sense of purpose. The abundant life He offers stands in stark contrast to a life that is marked by empty promises. Choices that reflect God's Will won't rob me like a thief in the night.

This summer, I attended the Taylor Swift Eras Tour multiple times. This is not a humble brag—or any brag of any kind. It was magical and memorable for many reasons. The most obvious reason was, of course, the Swifties. People from all walks of life made bracelets with letters that spelled out Swift's famous lyrics or songs. People would lean in to read the labels and make trades at the shows. I hopped on the trend and carefully selected titles I would wear proudly. I didn't want to be the Antihero. *I already bear this label deep down—I don't need it stretched across my wrist.* These bracelets felt as though they had the potential to expose my identity.

I'd like to invite you to join me in reclaiming our identities. Let's create bracelets that tell our redemption story. *Saved. Forgiven. Healed. Survivor.* Let's choose words that are meaningful and personal to us. When people ask, we have one more way to share God's amazing grace. We can give them to others as if to say, "I see this in you, too." A restored identity reminds us of God's goodness.

Take it to Heart

- What does an abundance mindset mean to you?

- Have you experienced a connection to God's Truth? Take time to reflect.

- How has God influenced your identity? What word(s) would you wear as labels (in reference to identity bracelets)?

Take it to God

- Read the description of verses on page 42 (Sections: *Our Relationship with God* and *Our New Identity*). What stands out as an area you are seeking Truth in your life today? Find the verse(s) in the Bible and invite God to restore this area.

4

Intentional Rest

I often save my farm chores for nightfall because I love to be out in the quiet darkness. Snow-covered earth bathed in moonlight is my favorite. The snow reflects the light, and I can see everything. Nothing is hidden, although nothing is out at that time. The raccoons, coyotes, and skunks are tucked away from the cold. This means they are not terrorizing my flock—or me—and I can move at my own pace. Occasionally, the deer will peer back at me, but they are so silent that I hardly notice them. My breath swirls out in steamy circles. The snow crunches and sparkles as I make my way through it.

The earth is resting under a winter blanket. The trees release their leaves, plants cast their seeds, and the ground has time to gather nutrients. Some creatures move on to warmer places, knowing they cannot survive in this climate. Others instinctively find a place to hibernate. In the snow-padded silence, nature enters into a deep sleep.

I find rest in winter, too. I don't have a green thumb, so while I attempt to grow as a farmer—it does not come naturally. It requires effort to prune the landscape, sow seeds, and reap a harvest. At the same time, my kids are home for the summer, and I want them to have equal parts fun and relaxation to look back on. Their break is my busy season. Between writing this book and entertaining my crew, I have completely neglected my flowerbeds. I have taken the title literally and spent my time out of the garden. Fall will provide structure, but winter will slow things down. I will be wearing my sweatpants and a hoodie by the time it arrives.

While scarcity thinking pushes us to *be more*, an abundance mindset calls us to *rest more*. We avoid wearing ourselves out by taking time to slow down and reflect. The more energy we exert, the more rest is required. In his study of scarcity, Shahram Heshmat, Ph.D. states, "Research suggests that the best way to get more done in less time requires one to avoid exhaustion and skillfully manage energy by getting sufficient sleep (eight or more hours), more breaks, or daytime naps."[7] Even science backs up our need for rest—and science never sleeps!

Intentional Rest
The world's model of rest is self-care, so let's distinguish the difference between this and intentional rest. Self-care is often a response to an over-stimulated life. We are looking for a break or something to make us feel good. Pedicures, massages, and retreats are all things we continue enjoying if time and money

allow. But that's just it—they require us to sacrifice our resources, which may not be sustainable over time. They take something away from you. When rest becomes consumerism, we lose access to it.

We are talking about something different here. By rest, I mean intentional rest. Sabbath. Shavat. It looks less busy and emphasizes the importance of connection, relationships, and purposeful living. God demonstrated Sabbath rest at the end of the first week of human existence (Gen. 2:3). Our Eternal Creator did not require rest—He modeled it for our benefit. This communicates to me that rest is not about limitations or weakness but points to something greater than itself.

In this chapter, we will focus on intentional rest. When your mind is tired, your heart is anxious, or you don't have the luxury of time—these are for you. There are times when we simply need to rest and reflect. We may not have the capacity for a deep theological study. We may have just enough in us to say, "Okay, Lord. I'm here." I think that's a pretty great start.

Sabbath
The Sabbath is mentioned over one hundred times throughout biblical history. This rest day is holy, blessed, a covenant, a reminder of freedom, a delight, and an act of obedience (Ex. 31:12-18). It is meant to set aside and honor God. We can do this through church attendance, whatever that looks like. While ideally, we would meet together, we have many ways to connect virtually.

Jesus practiced the Sabbath by praying, teaching, and healing. The Pharisees watched Him closely, constantly critiquing *how* He observed the Sabbath. In Luke 6:5, Jesus told them that He *is the Lord* of the Sabbath. He reminded them that this day was meant for doing good. Jesus simplified the matter by focusing on the *intention* behind practicing the Sabbath, not the *method* of practice. Measuring our motives requires humility, vulnerability, and honesty. It requires the courage to look within and consider change. Once again, Jesus brings it back to the heart and wants only what is genuine.

Our Father
When we read the Bible, it's helpful to depict God as a Father relating to His children. In the Old Testament, it appears that He adjusts the way He relates to each generation. I envision a new Father correcting His child for the first time. He tried everything to reach the hearts of His beloved. *In the beginning*, He created everything with a purpose. He walked with man in the Garden. He went on to perform grand miracles.

God chose ordinary people and gave them extraordinary stories. He equipped the minds of mortals to prophesy Jesus' arrival. God sent the Holy Spirit to move us from within. *In the beginning*, He knew Jesus would be the rescue plan. Even knowing how the story would end, God still felt emotional disappointment, anger, and sadness towards mankind for choosing sin over Him. His heart continues to ache for the way sin separates us from Him. That does not stop our Redeemer from empowering our faith to be shared with others.

What if we viewed the Sabbath with the same reverence as Father's Day? What are some of the Father's Day traditions you've observed in your family or others? What makes a dad feel special? He may prefer a favorite meal, a small gift, or quality time together. The pace of the day matches his wants and needs. The Sabbath takes another meaning when we consider God in this way. It is a weekly Father's Day, a time to prioritize Dad and celebrate Him.

In the same way, the Sabbath is meant to celebrate who God has been to you and offer your precious time to be with Him. It is an opportunity to reflect on how God has provided for you in the past while believing He hasn't given up on you yet. It doesn't matter how you hold your fork or if you eat with your hands. You do not have to say the *right thing*. Sabbath is meant to be shared, so break bread with friends and family. This time to rest revitalizes us. I picture plugging into an endless power supply. Our low battery light is suddenly green, and we have renewed energy to complete the work ahead.

God as our Father is loaded with meaning for each of us. We inadvertently compare God to our dads, using an earthly example for what we cannot see. Some of our fathers were attentive and kind. It is through their tenderness we know their love for us. Some of our fathers pushed us, wanting the best and challenging us to do more. Others were distant, unwilling, or unsure of how to connect. Still, others were cruel, the thought of them unbearable to recall. I know this list only includes some of the complexities of this relationship.

I want you to imagine a box and label it "Dad." Think about your father and some words you'd use to describe him. Put those labels in the box. This perspective shapes the way you experience your dad. Now place the container in God's hands. God is not limited to the labels inside that box. He knows the roots of your dad's shortcomings. He knit you and your father together, separately created but relationally intertwined. What would it feel like to release your dad, to let go of the box? Your boundaries are still important, but they are ever more present as you distinguish between you and him, him and God. When you picture your dad in God's hands, it is easier to pray for his frailty and your own. The Lord offers the same grace to both you and your father.

The difference between your dad and our Father is unfailing love. Parents are limited to the conditions of humanity, while God is more dynamic than we can imagine. We desire the type of acceptance from our parents that flows endlessly from our Creator's heart. He multiplies our Sabbath offering of time and obedience into a fruitful spirit. He takes our rest and turns it into success. Not the kind of success that turns the world's head. He offers a wealth of peace, a beautiful heart, and abundant grace. His light shines through the character that develops as we grow closer to Him.

Prayer
Every healthy relationship relies on communication in order to grow deeper and closer to one another. Prayer is a way to express gratitude, confession, love, and adoration. We use it to seek wisdom and help. We can use prayer to express *anything at all*. It is meant to be vulnerable and genuine, a conversation between love and beloved. As we grow in this relationship, we experience familiarity and connection. A praying mind will instinctively call out to the Lord when it feels uneasy. Our responses form patterns based on what we believe is working. If prayer leads to peace or clarity, we are more likely to call out the next time we require relief.

Second Corinthians 9:8 (ESV) says, "And God is able to make all grace abound to you, so that having all sufficiency in all things at all times, you may abound in every good work." When I hear the word "abound," and I don't hear it often, it makes me think of overgrowth, overflowing, overjoyed, *Over the Top*, backward-hat-style, as it goes beyond what is reasonable or expected (Thank you, Sylvester Stallone, circa 1987).[8]

God has the omnipotence to make our lives flourish in the overflowing well of His grace. He has *all the grace*. He has the omniscience to prepare good works for us, individually and with care. His good works often go beyond what we could imagine on our own. He could make food and water materialize essentially out of thin air, so imagine how much more He can do with a willing heart. He specializes in the unseen.

Jesus modeled the importance of prayer in His ministry. He often prayed alone, which displays the intimacy and confidentiality we can experience in our prayer life. Hebrews 5:7 tells us that Jesus prayed with tears and loud crying. This emotional expression gives us a glimpse of the kinship between Father and Son. Jesus could go to His Father for anything. We can easily conclude that God is empathic and longs to know our hearts. When Jesus bridged the gap, He made this relationship possible for us, too. When we allow Jesus to remove the layer of sin between us and God, we can see Him more clearly.

Below are more examples of Jesus' prayer life:

- He prayed for believers (John 17:9, 20)
- He prayed for the faith and ministry of His followers (Luke 22:32)
- He prayed after being baptized, which demonstrated submission to God's design, and invited the Holy Spirit into the picture (Luke 3:21, 22)
- He prayed for His enemies (Luke 5:44)
- He offered to pray on our behalf and encouraged a relationship with the Holy Spirit (John 14:16)
- He taught people how to pray (Matthew 6:9-14)

These verses represent a snapshot of Jesus' ministry. How on earth do I narrow down the greatest hits to a simple bullet list? It simply does not do Him justice. The Bible is filled with accounts of His ministry. You'll just have to read for yourself, I suppose (read with a wink and a smile).

The Lord's Prayer
I have spent most of my life hearing the Lord's Prayer repeated in a monotonous tone. Public readings often lack enthusiasm, *am I right?* I have viewed them more as acts of obedience than words that bond me to the Lord. At the same time, I trust that Jesus' example was both perfect and applicable. Finding new ways to connect is refreshing, but is not meant to replace what already works. Jesus' format for prayer is both tried and true.

Scripture presents reliable staples when it comes to spiritual growth and development. If our prayer life grows stagnant, we can revive it with Jesus' prayer. I can't think of a better way than to return to the source. Jesus offered a template in Matthew 6:9-13 (ESV) when He told us to pray this way:

> "Our Father in heaven, hallowed be Your name. Your kingdom come, Your will be done, on earth as it is in heaven. Give us this day our daily bread, and forgive us our debts, as we also have forgiven our debtors. And lead us not into temptation, but deliver us from evil."

In Figure 2, I've broken these verses down into five sections. This is not meant to reduce Christ's words—only to illustrate an important concept.

Figure 2

PRAY THIS *Way*

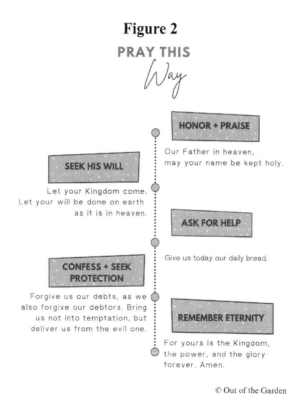

HONOR + PRAISE
Our Father in heaven, may your name be kept holy.

SEEK HIS WILL
Let your Kingdom come. Let your will be done on earth as it is in heaven.

ASK FOR HELP
Give us today our daily bread.

CONFESS + SEEK PROTECTION
Forgive us our debts, as we also forgive our debtors. Bring us not into temptation, but deliver us from the evil one.

REMEMBER ETERNITY
For yours is the Kingdom, the power, and the glory forever. Amen.

© Out of the Garden

Let's take a closer look at this prayer:

- **Honor and Praise:** Jesus begins by honoring God. Our gaze immediately shifts to His holiness. Prayer starts with humility and respect. Beginning with recognition reminds us to place our desires in His hands, measuring their value against His vision. I am less likely to make demands when I begin this way. How do we praise God? How do we glorify His name?

- **Seek His Will:** Acknowledging God's sovereignty, Jesus shows us how to invite heavenly influence into our lives. There is submission in laying down the blueprints for your kingdom. What are some ways you can invite His Kingdom into your life? In what ways are you building a separate empire?

- **Ask for Help:** By asking God for provision, we trust that He will respond. We can boldly ask that He would provide for our daily needs, just as He offered manna to the Israelites (Ex. 16:32-34). What needs do you have today? How can you present them to God?

- **Confess and Seek Protection:** Pray for your enemies. Forgive people that have hurt you. We can approach the Father directly and honestly. Confession reminds us of our imperfections, which makes us more empathic. Receiving mercy softens our hearts to extend it to others. By acknowledging our thoughts and feelings toward others, we make room for change. Who do you need to forgive today? Who will you pray for, despite the hurt they have caused?

- **Remember Eternity:** Our gaze returns to the Lord. We can rely on His steadfast love and unfailing power. Our circumstances are temporary. With our eyes fixed on forever, the worries of this world slip through our fingers like sand through the hourglass of time.

I will most likely spend this entire lifetime submitting certain thoughts and beliefs to God. He gently nudges me to pray for my enemies, express gratitude in place of complaints, and confess my part in conflict and disillusionment. I am reminded in my humility that a tender heart has a greater capacity for love. It is also glaringly apparent that these changes are temporary. Like Vitamin C, my body requires a regular dose of His grace because it is not stored away for later use. My heart and soul need a regular dose of Vitamin G. *I'm sorry. I had to do it.* I cannot force change or pretend to be something I am not. And neither can you. *What a relief.* Ultimately, I am learning to pray that He will transform my life as only He can.

There is Power in Jesus' Name

I have seen on multiple occasions the power of praying Jesus' name. Not long ago, our family visited an amusement park. While my daughter and I waited in line for the chair swings, a little boy ran right up to us with big crocodile tears streaming down his cheeks. I looked around for someone who might be looking for him, but couldn't find anyone. His screams grew louder as I tried to talk to him. My heart repeatedly felt the words "*pray for him.*" So I knelt down and asked God to show him that He loves and protects him. As soon as I said Jesus' name, *that boy was silent.* He looked me right in the eye. It was powerful. I continued to say Jesus' name as I prayed for this boy to feel loved and safe. After praying, I asked if he knew how much God loved him, and he shook his head no. I told him he could say Jesus' name to help him whenever he felt scared, sad, or alone.

The boy was calm as he got on the ride, occasionally looking back at my daughter and me. He returned to his party, and we saw him around the park that day. While I don't expect this to have transformed his life, I hope it contributes to his faith. Praying Jesus' name is *not* a parlor trick and certainly isn't foolproof. It is a proclamation of faith, a hand extended into the darkness, and calling out with the belief that there will be a response.

This is not the first time I have witnessed the peace that comes over someone when Jesus is invited into the conversation. In these instances, it was as though an alarm was triggered, and no one had the code. I watched fear burst out of them in tearfulness and distorted thoughts. As people began to pray in Jesus' name, the frenzy in their eyes disappeared and they could make eye contact. It was as though they could finally hear me or others that were with us. Gasping breaths slowed to a steady rhythm. It is hard to look away when this shift takes place.

Jesus became the filter which God sees us through, removing the labels of sin and shame. Our Father views us through His Son's eyes, which is a valuable perspective. He walked among us. He knows the frailty of our bodies and minds. In John 16:27 (ESV), Jesus says, "For the Father himself loves you, because you have loved me and have believed that I came from God." Jesus used prayer to silence our fears and demonstrate God's strength. Even as the Prince of Peace, He exemplified submission and servitude to humanity.

Worship

Have you noticed that music holds memories? A song can transport us to a different time or place, as though that memory is a holograph playing out before us. It is the closest I've come to time travel. Capable of sparking emotion and nostalgia, music is powerful. In the same way, worship impacts our relationship with God.

Whatever your style or genre, Christian artists are popping up in all of them. Many songs can encourage our faith, even if the chorus is vague or repetitive. Artists often incorporate Scripture in their stanzas. There have been times I am reading the Bible, and suddenly a chorus plays in my head—*I've heard this before.* The melodic version envelopes my mind, folding away the Truth with care. I now have more than one way to know these words by heart.

Music is often shared, so these songs may be playing in the background of your busy life. We can do two things at once, allowing God into the rhythm of our hustle. With repetition and familiarity, we begin to raise our voices together. Few things are sweeter than hearing little voices belting out faith-building lyrics from the backseat. We enjoy music in our house, but ultimately I want my kids to repeat the words that will strengthen their faith and confidence in the Lord.

Love Grows in Quiet Places

One of the most enchanting results of a heart filled by God is that love pours out of it. As I draw near to Him, He blesses my other relationships. I find richness in my friendship and love for my husband. I slow down and enjoy my kids. *I can let go of productivity and just be present.* I wish these moments could last forever, but for now, they are the sweet interludes.

His love repairs the parts of me that struggle with trust, forgiveness, and feeling content. Like a dad holding the back of the bicycle seat, He runs with me until I am steady. It may appear He has let go, but He is always nearby. I will hit the curb, fall, and land in the grass. I may throw the bike, kick the tires, or say a few choice words. *I'm suddenly reminded of training my boys to ride their bikes.* It's my job to find balance and pay attention to where I'm going. I have a choice to get back up and ride my bike to Him. He never left.

Take it to Heart

- What are some of your favorite ways to find intentional rest?

- What does God as a Father mean to you?

- What new information have you gained from this chapter? How will you apply it to your faith journey?

Take it to God

- Read 2 Corinthians 9:8 — Express gratitude for God's eternal, unfailing qualities.

5

Intentional Growth

Over the years, I have pursued a more intimate relationship with God. I struggled to fit in with the Bible study crowd. After our first miscarriage, I experienced extreme social anxiety that made it difficult for me to participate. I would walk into a room, look at friendly and familiar faces, and run straight to the bathroom to cry. The vulnerability left me feeling emotionally bankrupt. As a young mom, I didn't feel as though I had the capacity to go very deep into the Word. Some studies felt like I was learning a different language. *Some studies literally expect you to learn a different language.* It took time to find resources that allowed me to grow at my own pace.

I needed more direction and purpose in my quiet time. I knew it was necessary but I needed help with boredom, discipline, and time management. My unplanned prayer life led to a lack of commitment on my part. Should I crack my Bible open and read the words randomly? Would a study be helpful? In the quiet hours before everyone awoke, what would prayer look like? Does writing it count? Also, does worship count? How long should it take? Should I use a commentary? Should I learn Hebrew?

The answer is yes. And no, specifically to the "shoulds," because they aren't welcome here. Freedom and "should" are not harmonious together. Imagine approaching a friendship with these questions. You have a friend over at the same time every day. You invite them to your kitchen, living room, etc. You sit where you always sit because structure truly is a beautiful thing. You let the friend know what you'll discuss during this time. You may suggest how long you will be sitting together before you'd like the friend to go home so you can do other things. You speak in multiple languages, carefully checking the translation on your phone. You do most of the talking, ending your time with a list of requests you'd like the friend to accomplish and, if possible, in a timely manner.

This is ridiculous. It's robotic and unnatural. It is more an arrangement than a relationship. I, for one, would not come back. It seems ingenuine and self-serving. Sovereignty Himself is offering His wisdom and expertise in our lives, but often our schedules are already full. I know I have been guilty of overbooking and not surrendering my time.

God invites us into a relationship that has the power to transform our lives. He has the power to break through strongholds—addictions, unhealthy relationships, painful memories, etc. He offers relief from the pressure to be enough. This relationship drives us to be genuine. We grow out of the places we are fully known. His unconditional love offers refuge in an imperfect world.

For those of you raising little ones, I want to offer hope. I know how hard it is to spare another moment when you are already spread so thin. There were times I felt the Lord calling me to get out of bed in the darkest hours of the morning. *I did not always respond.* I would pull the *let's pray and see what happens* trick, resulting in me going back to sleep. When I did respond, I often felt as though my wick had been extended, even though it began burning so much earlier in the day. My heart was filled and prepared for the day in those still moments. Sleep is fantastic, but it couldn't do *that*. Thankfully, this has not been the case every morning.

My quiet time has changed so much over the years and continues to adapt to the changing needs of my family. The demands of motherhood have lessened as my kids have grown. Now they are old enough to stumble out of bed and cuddle up on the couch while I finish spending time with Jesus. By establishing the habit early on, they have grown to accept this as part of the routine. I had to fight for it and release myself of guilt for the days that it didn't work. The following list is not conclusive but includes some of my favorite approaches to understanding God more.

Praying the Bible
Praying the Bible is one of my favorite ways to connect with God. It is SO simple; literally, anyone can do it. You pick a chapter and read it line by line. With each line, you pray for whatever comes to mind. Don't overthink it. You pray whatever comes naturally. Sometimes you'll think of a random person

you want to pray for. Sometimes you'll apologize for that thing you said or did. You'll often thank Him that this is His word and that it's true. You'll ask the Lord for clarity on something that doesn't make sense. You may not find the answer you're looking for, but you are learning about God through the words He has shared. I believe God honors that. This approach is subjective, creating meaning for each of us individually.

In Donald S. Whitney's book, *Praying the Bible,* he distinguishes between praying and interpreting the Bible. He points to interpretation as *first* understanding what the text means and *then* praying for wisdom. Whitney asserts that praying the Bible is "merely using the language of the text to speak to God about what has come into your mind."[9] This method encourages us to respond naturally. Biblical interpretation is not the primary goal.

If you are looking for a place to begin, Whitney suggests the Psalms. Whitney says, "God gave the Psalms to us so that we would give the Psalms back to God. No other book of the Bible was inspired for that expressed purpose." I highly recommend this book to anyone seeking to learn more about this method. Several apps are also devoted to reading the Psalms, which can be easily read while waiting in line or just having a few moments to spare. I'm confident this approach will enrich your spiritual growth.

Journaling

In high school, I used writing to vent my frustrations. I was brutally honest as I scrawled out my words. Conflict in my family and confusion in relationships required an outlet, whether or not anyone else was talking about it. On the outside,

I was bubbly and talkative. I was screaming inside, reciting Papa Roach lyrics and begging for someone to pay attention. I used mod-podge to attach a black and white image of a girl running alone, titling the journal "My Darkest Days." *I was very emo.* I now read it with compassion for that part of me that ached for connection and healing.

As I read these journals now, I find that a ribbon of hope ties one entry to the next. They were not meant for worship or prayer, but my words revealed something beyond the agony. While I can still sense the anger that poured out of me, most pages ended with the anticipation that it would get better. God was present in my life in ways that I couldn't comprehend at the time. I felt raw and exposed, but I was still secure in His embrace. My brokenness never had the final say. In the midst of my darkest days, I had invited Jesus into my heart. I had not scared Him away. He was still there. *He still is today.* That presence has ignited a love for writing that brings me to these words on this page today.

A prayer journal is one of my absolute favorite spiritual practices. When I graduated from high school, a dear friend gave me a spiral-bound journal with a watercolor sheep on the front, which became my first prayer journal. I took that adorable collection of pages to college and wrote my prayers to God. I could speak loudly in my heart, firmly with my pen, and silently in my room as the busy dorm bustled around me. Prayer poured out of me—It felt like worship. Since then, I have filled many journals with prayers and praise. My journals are often where I record the results of praying the Word, word study, and meditation. I look back with nostalgia and see where God was faithful to me in each chapter of my story.

A prayer journal is pretty simple and straightforward. For me, it was an outlet that I could access at any time. It was entirely my own and I could say anything. I approached it with more intentionality than my writing journal. *And much less Papa Roach.* In a way, writing a prayer journal submitted my well-trained hand to point thoughts and feelings back to the Lord, allowing His influence to shape them.

I understand that only some people love to write. *Trust me.* I have two boys who have clearly expressed the "damaging effects" of handwritten words. We have a teacher gift budget for this very reason. I'm being facetious, of course, but I'm certain that some of you dislike writing as much as my boys. *It's not for everyone.*

For those that are open to it, journaling can be beneficial. Scientific research suggests that people recall handwritten concepts more accurately than those that are typed out. In the study, *The Benefits of Writing,* Dr. Smith, discovered that writing by hand can improve mental functioning and emotional regulation. Writing incorporates our ability to develop a thought and produce results.[10] We are in control. We may feel unruly, but our brains and bodies are engaged, proving they can work together.

Therapy often incorporates journaling because it allows clients to connect thoughts with feelings concretely. Abstract ideas find structure on the page. In seasons of grief and transition, writing can help you find clarity. A weary mind can find rest in prayer journaling. Rather than worrying about what to say, words flow freely and with the transparency of a diary. Writing can support our overall well-being.

Word Study

I learned about word study from a dear friend, Michelle Armstrong, who created a series called, *Encounters at the Feet of Jesus*. In six sessions, she demonstrated the mastermind of God and the masterpiece of Scripture by walking us through the miracles of Jesus. This friend enriched my faith through her example and the wisdom she shared over coffee or brunch. I will reference her study more than once because it is just that powerful.

When I think of word study, I think of a basket woven together. The story moves consistently through each word, and the author carefully considers their meaning and placement. Many words point to something beyond themselves, and repetition denotes importance. The words work together to create a pattern, holding Truth firmly in place. It strengthens my faith to see how God has entwined it so flawlessly.

Michelle noted that a word study can be helpful because it offers credibility, a timeline, geography, and multiple accounts of Truth across generations. Their stories are corroborated by the way they line up with one another. Michelle quipped, "You can't get that today on the news!"[11] We have incredible technology and access to many parts of the world. Even still, certainty seems to be elusive.

Encounters at the Feet of Jesus prompted participants to consider factors that would add context to Scripture. These included questions about the author (Who is the author? What do we know about them? Why'd they write it? What was their writing style?), when does it fall in the big Bible story timeline (Creation, the Fall, Redemption, Restoration), the meaning of words, and what was happening at that time (context based on other verses). Names and places suddenly took on new meaning. God's fingerprint was all over the lives of people I have read about as though they were simply extras in the presence of the main characters. In the Bible, there are no extras—their stories were *the real stories.* Jesus stepped into them to reveal purpose and wisdom. I imagine God delights in what appear to be coincidences.

A word study can be personalized and hand-crafted to suit your spiritual growth. The depth, length of time, and content are all up to you. You can keep a list of words you'd be interested in studying. Themes will likely emerge from the places we want to grow the most. There are many ways to find collections of topical and relatable verses. I often do an Internet search for lists of verses when I am beginning a word study.

Even with its simplicity, a word study can present some challenges. While it is open to interpretation, this way of reading Scripture can require more context and clarity. It is best used with an open mind and no agenda. You may end up on a rabbit trail, so hide the clock. Reading the original text of Scripture may lead to more questions. What on earth are they trying to say? The Gospel Coalition recommends six steps to avoid these pitfalls and develop a word study that offers depth and introspection:

1. **Pick the right word.** It goes without saying, but we are not looking at filler words. If, and, or but are meant to get us from one passage to the next. We are talking about descriptive words. Culturally specific words. Challenging words. *Things that make you go, hmmm.*

When we ask ourselves, "What does this word mean here?" we are on the right track.

2. **Find the Greek or Hebrew word.** With a quick web browse, I can find concordances, commentaries, apps, etc., that will direct me through the original text. The goal is not fluency, just interpretation. Some resources are more user-friendly than others, so shop around and find those that allow you to understand the text.

3. **Unearth other occurrences.** After finding the original word, we can explore its use in Scripture. How was this word used? When? But why? Use those detective skills to make connections and understand more fully.

4. **Note the range of possible meanings.** Have you heard the saying, "There's more than one way to skin a cat?" I have never understood a time or place that I would need to know even one way, but this saying has remained in my brain for all the years of my life. While we may interpret a word one way, another translation might suggest a completely different meaning. Exploring these ideas is essential. The content forms our values and beliefs, which will be expressed in our daily lives.

5. **Check with the commentators.** Any Joe Shmoe on the Internet can write a commentary. Find a reputable source that conveys Scripture truthfully and consistently. You can find arguments supporting or disproving almost anything on every corner of the web. A commentary is meant to be biblically sound and appropriately challenging when accurate to the Word.

6. **Make your decision.** Use the information you've gathered to make a choice. Consider the influence it has on your current outlook. Has anything changed? It may still be a gray area without a clear conclusion. In this case, you may hold your response loosely and quietly, open to further interpretation.[12]

Meditation
Meditation has become increasingly popular over the years. It connects our breath to our thoughts to remain present in the moment. This practice is coupled with mindfulness, allowing us to eliminate distractions by focusing on the moment. If I am eating a meal, I'm paying attention to the texture, taste, and other features of that food. In a conversation, I make eye contact, observe body language, and make a mental note of social cues. By remaining present, I am slowing down and taking in more information. Multitasking places a strain on our lives. Alternately, meditation effectively reduces the impact of stress and anxiety by combating intrusive thoughts. Not surprisingly, it is a helpful therapeutic intervention, as well.

Research suggests that meditation can balance our systems, creating a greater sense of well-being. According to Forbes Health, "Mediation can improve your quality of life thanks to its many psychological and physical benefits."[13] It promotes mental health by using practices that support the nervous system. Deep breathing and mindfulness reduce the physical symptoms of stress and worry. For example, anxiety can produce symptoms that resemble a heart attack: tingling, racing heart, sweating, etc. When meditation is used to calm the nervous system, it reduces these symptoms. It allows the body to successfully regulate emotions.

When the body experiences relief from stress or mood disturbances, it can lower blood pressure, strengthen the immune system, and alter how you respond emotionally. The advantages of a harmonious system include improved memory, better sleep, and healthy self-awareness. Meditation soothes our internal systems, connects us more deeply to ourselves, and can also deepen our relationship with God.

A simple word study of the Bible reveals that breath is used to describe the places God brings life (Gen. 2:7) and death (2 Thess. 2:8), renewing the spaces in between (Job 33:4). Meditation allows us to combine the tradition of Eastern practices with our desire to be present with the Lord. I believe God has given us something as essential and elemental as breathing to calm our minds. Meditation is meant to offer more than momentary relief or improved daily functioning. It is the epitome of intentional rest. We can claim the words of Isaiah 26:3 (NIV) back to God: "You will keep in perfect peace those whose minds are steadfast, because they trust in you." Some practical ways to adopt meditation in your faith journey include the following:

- Seeking insight and wisdom (Psalm 49:3)
- To experience healing (Proverbs 4:20-22)
- Applying truth to our lives (Joshua 1:8)
- Focusing on good things (Philippians 4:8)
- Searching our hearts (Psalm 139:23, 24)
- Glorifying God with our lives (Psalm 19:14)
- Deepening our obedience (Psalm 119:15)
- Remembering God's faithfulness (Psalm 77:12)
- Growing to love and adopt the Word daily (Psalm 119:48)

The beauty of meditation is that it is accessible to all. It requires no spiritual training. Meditation often includes focusing on a specific verse or attribute of God, slowly consuming each word with each breath. I often breathe in the words of Truth and breathe out the lie I've attached to them, disentangling the two. The words flow in and out of my mind like a mental housekeeper brushing away the cobwebs. Meditating allows me to hone in on the observations presented by Scripture and try to understand them further. Practically speaking, this is a quick and easy way to implement this habit. Guided meditation is a great way to take it a step further and promote spiritual benefits.

Guided Meditation
Find a comfortable, quiet place to begin. Place your hands, palms facing up, on your lap. This symbolic posture suggests you are open to what God will share. Take a deep breath in for four seconds, hold it, and release it for six seconds. Do this three times and notice how your body begins to relax. Imagine a scanner moving over your body, stopping where you are holding tension. Begin with your neck and move down each part of the body, flexing and releasing where you feel tension. Ask God to be present in this moment and help you to focus and gain insight. For example, you might pray, "Lord, please help me to let go of this thought/belief/idea." Imagine your body relaxing and releasing the muscle. Continue to scan the rest of your body. Take a deep breath in, hold it, and release it.

Now think of the verse, attribute, or other truth you want to meditate on. Slowly consider each word. What comes to mind? Do you experience gratitude? Offer thanks to God. Is there a necessary change needed in your life? Does it call for confession? Compassion? Healing? Renewal? Take a moment to apply the insight to your life. Breathe in deeply as you ask God to increase your understanding. Do this with each word or attribute. Continue until you have a sense of peace and clarity. Thank God for being present in this moment. Slowly open your eyes as you return to normal breathing. Figure 3 provides a visual to easily practice guided meditation on your own.

Figure 3

GUIDED MEDITATION

01 Get comfortable, with palms facing up on lap

02 3X—Breathe in for 4, out for 6

03 Scan your body for tension

04 Ask God to be present

05 Focus—what comes to mind?

06 Apply insight to life

07 Express gratitude for insight

© Out of the Garden

Connecting With God

Connecting with God is meant to draw us closer to our Creator, not prove ourselves in any way. Ephesians 2:8-10 (ESV) tells us that, "For by grace you have been saved through faith. And this is not your own doing; it is the gift of God, not a result of works, so that no one may boast. For we are his workmanship, created in Christ Jesus for good works, which God prepared beforehand, that we should walk in them." God's grace is a gift with no strings attached. Spending time with Him does not check a box or fulfill a requirement. Taking time to understand God more is a way to show humble gratitude and a vulnerable heart. Not only does He restore us, but He presents us to the world as His handiwork. We are carefully crafted and valued by Him. He has already established the good things that will result from this restoration.

As you begin to know Him more clearly, He will help you comprehend yourself more, as well. Psalm 37:4 (ESV) says, "Delight yourself in the Lord, and he will give you the desires of your heart." My interpretation is that He will not give us what we want or crave. *He is not Amazon Prime.* These words tell us that He knows us intimately and designed us to be loved. He knows every hurt, every wound, every aching memory. God knows that some of our wants were born out of a deficit of needs. He knows if they'll keep us there. He protects the places we need to grow. The Lord also recalls how we've felt loved, cherished, and seen. *He knows.* When we practice quiet restoration with Jesus, we find our identity in Him. We can let go of excessive striving. Our search for love and meaning is satisfied in Christ. Our original question shifts a bit. ***I could be known for this—but will Christ be known through this?***

Take it to Heart

- What are some of the ways you have connected with God in the past?

- What practices have you considered using in this chapter? What might that look like?

Take it to God

- Read one of the verses about meditation on page 73. How can you apply this to an area in your life?

- Meditate on this verse. Take deep breaths as you say each word.

- Offer it as a prayer and seek wisdom from the Lord.

6

What's Holding You Back?

I'd like to ask you a difficult question. In a perfect world, I would look you in the eye and express my compassion in this. You would know the motive of my heart by my posture in your presence. What I really want to ask is this: *What is holding you back from connecting with God?*

There are many answers. I have fallen prey to busyness, lack of focus, disobedience, and sin. It feels like such an open wound to lay before you, but I know I'm not alone. You may feel uncertain about spending time with God. Perhaps nothing is holding you back *now*, but it has in the past. Ask yourself what is preventing you from creating these habits of connection. Are there pitfalls or blind spots in your life? We often do not advertise these areas in our lives. While it may feel like a bold, neon sign points out our struggles, we keep them to ourselves. There are conversations we'd like to have but we recognize they are perceived as socially unacceptable. You may still be questioning if a relationship with God is something you are interested in—that alone may be the wall that stands between you and Him. As we continue, ask yourself if any of the following have stood in the way of your developing faith.

Disbelief
Let's get right to it. Disbelief is one of the greatest barriers to pursuing a relationship with God. It feels obvious to type and uncomfortable to address. Not having all the answers makes us feel sweaty and weak. Questions about the existence of God or the quality of His character are a big *no, thank you,* for me. When I describe the evidence of God's goodness and His presence in my life, I can almost sense the posture of my doubting friends turning to pity and concern. *Sweet girl*, their eyes read. *How foolish.* The reality is that many people do not believe in God—and will not after reading this book. *That's my time, folks.*

I began this section with the idea that our goal is to eradicate disbelief. I viewed it as an affront to ministry, a flaw in the system. I also viewed it through an archaic black-and-white filter, like an old movie without sound. If my goal is to write a book that's a bridge, then I want to do more good than harm. I won't suggest that you try harder or pray more. I'd rather provide a breadcrumb trail that you can follow, one step at a time, and decide for yourself if this is the path for you. Christianity must seem bewildering when it does not align with a personal worldview. You or someone you know may feel torn between the opposing truths of the world and Scripture. Believing in what you cannot see may not come naturally— especially when what you see is a world full of disarray. *How could a loving hand create this place and watch it crumble?* It may appear that God has dealt carelessly with Creation.

Disbelief can result from a negative experience in a church or with someone who claims to be a believer. *Christians continue to turn people away from Christianity.* We cannot automatically assume this discomfort is based on conviction. There are church-goers that leave the Gospel where they found it. Why would an unbelieving world take time out of its busy schedule to seek a God that people are leaving at the door?

There are also strange practices and dogmatic rituals that could distract from the main message. If it is not your cultural norm, it may feel abnormal. In high school, a group of us attended my friend's church, which was drastically different from our own. It was loud, charismatic, chaotic, and in-your-face. We were so uncomfortable that we ended up hanging out (aka hiding) in a back room until our friend was ready to leave. This is not meant to critique their practices, but to acknowledge that churches are not one-size-fits-all. Each of us had a home church to which we could return. However, this is not the case for everyone. An awkward experience on its own can leave you vowing never to return to a church building.

I believe disbelief is also closely linked to disappointment. Belief is built on trust, so it stands to reason that a person has felt let down in some way. Unmet expectations are often linked to questions about God's existence. Faith becomes a sign of weakness, an unrequited hope. We may know it by some other name—pride, self-sufficiency, or personal strength. Does the crushing weight of disappointment cause you to hide your heart from further damage?

At its core, disbelief—or doubt, unbelief, discontent, discord, etc.—is deeply protective. It may be a conscious choice to *not turn out like that guy.* It is fueled by logical, concrete thinking. In my experience, people who deny Christian living are motivated by tangible evidence, their eyes drawn to the world around them. In a way, they're right. They are following our gaze. The Gospel ultimately resides in the church body today. If we as believers have also fixed our eyes on the world, then why would a skeptic ever look up?

Our best response to disbelief is ultimately grace. Allow others to figure out for themselves, in their own time. God transforms hearts quietly, like a seed planted in soil. If He can wait patiently, then we do not need to hurry things along. It's not our job to remove the seed from the ground, pry it open, and demand that life springs out of it. Instead, we water and feed it. Fertilizer—a collection of dead things (yum) that provide nutrients—is the best way to grow new things. The fertilizer in our lives may include the places we've surrendered, the struggles we've overcome, and the peace beyond understanding. Only God can take what is dead and reuse it. Our faith grows in those transformative moments, so what prevents us from sharing them with the world?

Belief calls us to keep our eyes focused on eternity. In Philippians 3:1-11, Paul shares his reasons for his faith. He credits his righteousness to His confidence in Christ. He experienced a powerful change of heart that motivated his ministry. Like Paul, I find that it's helpful to review any evidence that supports my belief in that moment. Previous experiences, unexplainable coincidences, and the consistency of Truth draw my mind away from the edge of uncertainty.

Paul expresses his desire to know Christ—His life, death, and resurrection. In Philippians 3:12-14 (NIV), he says, "Not that I have already obtained all this, or have already arrived at my goal, but I press on to take hold of that for which Christ Jesus took hold of me. Brothers and sisters, I do not consider myself yet to have taken hold of it. But one thing I do: Forgetting what is behind and straining toward what is ahead, I press on toward the goal to win the prize for which God has called me heavenward in Christ Jesus." I've claimed this passage since high school—it was listed alongside my senior yearbook photo and posted over the mirror of my first dorm room door. I resonated with the humility of not having all of the answers, but never giving up. Moments of doubt or uncertainty do not discredit my belief. They are part of the faith journey, not a closed road or failed detour. I may not be a runner, but I'm also not a quitter. Regardless of my flaws or queries, I do my best to let go of anxiety and worry to focus on the finish line. I long to hear the words, "Well done, good and faithful servant" (Matt. 25:21, NIV).

At the end of the day, our faith cannot be based on other people. There are wolves among us, strategically placed to lead prey away from the flock. Instead, we are called to become so familiar with His Word that we are instantly aware of lies that aim to tear us down or pull us away. We are encouraged as the author of Hebrews 10:22-25 says, "Let us draw near to God with a sincere heart and with the full assurance that faith brings, having our hearts sprinkled to cleanse us from a guilty conscience and having our bodies washed with pure water. Let us hold unswervingly to the hope we profess, for He who promised is faithful. And let us consider how we may spur one another on toward love and good deeds, not giving up meeting together, as some are in the habit of doing, but encouraging one another—and all the more as you see the Day approaching."

Injustice
Injustice is ever-present in our world today. Arrogance and selfishness drive people to pursue personal gain, resulting in oppressed and marginalized people. It's a foreign concept to our created purpose, which included clearly defined roles and walking unencumbered alongside the Creator. Adam and Eve were the first sojourners, separated from God and no longer welcome in the place they called home. While the punishment fit the crime, their choice resulted in years of inequality and confusion for years to come. Sin wreaks havoc on our original design.

Howard Thurman
To gain perspective, I dove into the biography of Howard Thurman, a black pioneer in the social justice movement. Thurman grew up in the segregated South with a mother who spoke Truth over his life. Thurman was a lonely child who found comfort in nature, often meditating on God's presence there. He understood the value of education and became the first African American to complete the eighth grade. Thurman went on to become valedictorian of his high school and college. In 1949, he wrote *Jesus and the Disinherited* in response to oppression. He saw the parallels between the life of Jesus and modern-day untouchables. As a friend and mentor to Martin Luther King, Jr., Thurman influenced the practice of non-violent protests. Thurman responded to injustice with faith and fortitude. He did not call himself a missionary but tended to the marginalized people of the world.

In the documentary, *Backs Against the Wall: The Howard Thurman Story*, Jesse Jackson noted that "He came to defend the poor. To live with the needy. To set the captive free."[14] Thurman modeled his life after that of Christ and broke through barriers. He founded The Fellowship Church For All People—the first multiracial, intergenerational church. After Martin Luther King, Jr. was stabbed, Howard visited him in the hospital and suggested a time of rest to reflect. After taking this advice, King, Jr. wrote the book, *Where Do We Go From Here?* It became a farewell piece and a cherished legacy as he was assassinated soon after. Without the influence and faith of his mentor, Howard, we might not have this treasure today.

Injustice occurs when someone is taken advantage of and their rights are revoked. It is the consequence of someone else's choice. Our experiences with this are spread out across a spectrum, but the bottom line remains the same—we didn't ask for this. It's tempting to feel angry toward God or believe He's failed us in some way.

At the root, blaming God is a defense mechanism. It's meant to serve as a coping skill but does not offer relief. Flooded emotions make it difficult to recall negative experiences accurately. Our confusion does not discredit the validity of the incident but suggests that some memories are so agonizing that our minds will work hard to protect us from them. A trigger is the body's way of storing what happened, responding even when our mind has lost track of the details.

Some trauma requires the assistance of a mental health professional. Our emotions and physiological responses to stressors are our bodies' communication methods. A trained professional can help navigate them and provide alternate responses. We are not minimizing our pain. We are not labeling it as God's oversight. We are not staying in a place where we feel abandoned and forgotten. By removing blame or other unhelpful coping mechanisms, we acknowledge the pain we experienced, place responsibility where it is due, and be honest with ourselves about moving forward.

The Bible is full of people facing insurmountable odds and painful circumstances. Their responses ranged from emotional expression to personal submission. You may find comfort in reading their stories and seeing their humanity amid it all. Of course, they felt angry, scared, uncertain, or broken-hearted. Of course, they struggled with their belief. Of course, they wanted to give up. Of course, you sometimes want to, as well.

Joseph
One story of injustice that readily comes to mind is that of Joseph (Genesis 37-50). I will note the highlights, but I highly recommend reading the entire story for yourself. Joseph was favored by his father, Jacob, which caused his brothers to hate him. Joseph interpreted dreams that involved his family bowing before him, which did not go over well. They stripped Joseph of an ornate robe Jacob had given him and sold him into slavery. He was purchased and rapidly promoted to the chief attendant in Potiphar, an Egyptian leader's, household. Potiphar's wife could not convince Joseph to sleep with her, so she stole his cloak and lied to her husband about advances Joseph had not actually made. Joseph was thrown in prison, where he once again advanced and now served alongside the warden.

He accurately interpreted the visions of Pharaoh's cupbearer and baker, both imprisoned. The cupbearer was reinstated but forgot Joseph. It was not until Pharah required discernment for his own dreams that the cupbearer remembered Joseph. Joseph revealed his wisdom to Pharaoh by accurately depicting a season of abundance followed by scarcity. Pharaoh placed Joseph as second-in-command of Egypt and dressed him in fine linen robes. Joseph created a plan to store goods that fed Egyptians and surrounding nations. Which brings us to his family.

Joseph's brothers came to Egypt for grain and did not recognize their brother. By my interpretation, he witnessed the burden they must have carried for years after what they had done to Joseph. In time, he revealed his identity and provided for his family. He was reunited with Jacob before his death. Joseph's story is an example of character when it matters the most. He responded to his brothers with uncommon goodness. Joseph was clothed in favor, of slavery, imprisonment, and authority. His identity did not depend on his attire, though. *Joseph was clothed in God's grace and provision.* Joseph was able to succeed and experience victory as a result of his faithfulness to the Lord.

Howard and Joseph have one thing in common—they never gave up. We cannot control our circumstances, but we can control how we respond to them. When our identity is stabilized securely in the Master's hands, we are not smashed and thrashed by the troubles we face. It takes courage to be humbled in this way.

Triggers

Let's take a moment to differentiate emotions from triggers. Our culture uses the two interchangeably, creating a disadvantage when evaluating pain and suffering. We can usually find the connection between our emotions and our thoughts or beliefs. While we may be caught off-guard by our emotions, we usually think about the situation as we are reacting to it. *That person annoys me. I don't like it when this happens. I don't want to be here.* It's normal to feel unsettled by our reactions or dislike how we feel. This response causes us to feel "activated" as we work through the discomfort. Activation is not necessarily related to a trigger.

A trigger, on the other hand, is a bodily response to trauma. It is a message from a past experience. It may activate an emotional response, but the trigger is automatic. The body developed it as a response to avoid danger and trauma. It feels like survival. When a person is safe, a trigger response is no longer valid. It may prevent future risks and limit a person's life unnecessarily.

A person might respond to triggers with firm boundaries—*I won't get hurt in that way again.* They may have difficulty forming boundaries—*I don't know how to stop this from happening.* It is common to avoid it altogether—*I will pretend this isn't happening.* Triggers are often associated with a sense of control, whether a person feels they have it or they do not.

When we expect others to respond to our triggers in specific ways, we create rules that make us feel safe. We are asking them to enable our behavior, not support our personal growth. I know—enable is a dirty word. I'll go a step further and say that valuing familiarity over compromise may lead to manipulation, gaslighting, coercion, and crazy-making. When our goal is to control, we are reactive rather than responsive.

Another running joke between my husband and I is that we 1) understand gaslighting, and 2) can detect it in TV shows or comments the other one makes. *We're a bundle of laughs.* Our weird determination to call it out leads to us pointing fingers as if to say, "Aha! I've caught you!" Truthfully, we are calling out the moments we perceive as genuine feelings being ignored, overlooked, or renamed to avoid responsibility. When we allow our triggers to call the shots, we may experience confused boundaries, damaged relationships, and isolation. By creating new interactions, we can disengage the triggers and experience healing.

I'm not suggesting we forgive and forget, put ourselves in dangerous situations, or do anything so cavalier. But I am challenging our expectations of others. We are not responsible for keeping each other in a "deactivated" state. We do not have to bear the burden of being likable or refined to their standard. While unfiltered words are often met with consequences, we are not required to walk on eggshells for fear of others' reactions. Appropriate boundaries and a safe environment help move us from a victim mentality to that of survival. Rewriting the story requires healing and a new response to triggers—*I may not be able to control this, but this is what I can do.* We focus on what is within our power in order to move on.

However, the key to letting go of hurt is forgiveness. The Bible is clear that accepting, loving, and following Christ results in freedom from sin. Our redemption is not in question. We do not promise perfection or pay off our debt. In Scripture, we are often directed to deal others the same gracious hand we have been dealt—forgiveness without strings. We carry the burden of unforgiveness while Jesus bore the entire weight of our sins. *All of our sins.* His grace extends to the furthest corners of the earth, as far as the east is from the west (Ps. 104:1). In His perfection, He performed the miracle of forgiveness so that we could experience it, too.

Lies
We have a complex dynamic with authority figures in our society. I will keep politics to a minimum, but I see public figures and leaders in roles meant to serve others. Those same officials can be influenced by money, power, and success. *I know. I was surprised when I learned this, too.* It is difficult to trust those we see, let alone a God we don't see. In our last election cycle, a wealth of misinformation influenced how people viewed our candidates. Research indicates that even after one exposure to a lie, it seems authentic.[15] The best way to avoid this influence is to first proactively avoid engaging with the information, which means limiting contact with faulty sources. It's a pre-strike—a pre-meditated detour. We avoid the bad neighborhoods where misinformation lives. The other response is to repeat the truth to replace the lie. Repetition will not eliminate the presence of the lie in our minds, but it will reduce its impact. They become less influential as we disengage with them.

As many lies exist about these candidates, there are thousands more about God. Even when it is corrected, the untruth lives on in the brain. It requires constant supervision to keep it from developing roots and outgrowing the truth. We can use the same principles of correction to solidify biblical concepts in our minds. Practically speaking, we pay attention to the information that goes in through our eyes and ears, stored away in our minds like computers.

When I think of the lies we believe, I often think of C.S. Lewis's book, *The Screwtape Letters*. It is a fictional account of an older demon mentoring a younger apprentice to patronize the human assigned to him. The format imitates letters exchanged as the more senior demon offers several ways to distract the person from following Christ, hoping he will fall into their wayward clutch. It is filled with poignant quotes that make you think. A favorite related to what we are discussing is this—"Prosperity knits a man to the world. He feels that he is finding his place in it, while really it is finding its place in him."[16] Lies about our time and what is valuable will prevent us from submitting to God's good, good will. If I were to write my own *Screwtape Letter* for us, it would read: "Place an image of perfection just out of their reach. By the time they realize they are lost, they will have wandered into our grasp." How often has a lie appeared beautiful, appealing, and satisfying—only to find out that it is not?

Our Sin

We are all sinners. We all know it, but it still feels offensive to begin here. *Don't mind me, as I find ways to make friends and influence people.* Starting here requires us to strip off our armor and stand vulnerably before the reality of our weakness. That sounds so scary. However, if we are honest with ourselves the armor has become very, very heavy. Sin begins with longing. It presents itself as the thing that will fill us and the satisfaction we desire. Our sin is shaped by past experiences, stories we've been told, our family of origin, our beliefs, and our influences. We are more prone to make choices that have been exhibited before us and continue those patterns. Our tendency to measure our lives against those around us makes some options look carefree, inconsequential, and, I dare say, fun. *It must be so nice to do whatever you want,* we think.

Our thoughts shape our attitudes, which shape our actions. Matthew 12:34 warns that our words will reflect the contents of our hearts. The thoughts and beliefs that fill our minds cannot help but pour out into our words and actions. Our perception solidifies with past experiences. *This feels like the truth because it has been true for me.* Without realizing it, we operate from a sense of entitlement. *I deserve this.*
Our sin, no matter how big or small, has the capacity to separate us from God and lead to shame. Shame tells us we are not _____ enough. It says we are wrong because _____. These labels fuel shame. Hating ourselves leads to a weakened resolve and isolation from others. We become vulnerable. Shame is a product of deceit—an exaggeration of what's true that prevents us from living authentically. It is a lonely battle for the mind.

Another element of sin is other people. *I would sin far less if they weren't around.* My tone is playful here, but in reality, it's true. The things I say and do that dishonor God are mostly relationally driven. Whether I worry about what someone thinks or feel proud of some success, it is often motivated by others. The problem is that we are all human, and not one of us has all the answers. We will get opposing information if we look to others to fulfill us. We will split ourselves into a million pieces in an effort to please everyone. *But we are not for everyone.* That's a tough pill to swallow as a Christian, as we have this odd belief that we need to be sunshine and smiles wherever we go. The Lord is not preoccupied with how we appear to others. He does not look at our outward appearance as man does (1 Sam. 16:7). He looks at our hearts with kindness. We are equipped with emotions, not bogged down by their presence.

Our Father wants to redeem us. John 1:5 (ESV) says, "The light shines in the darkness, and the darkness has not overcome it." No matter what we are facing, light can ALWAYS break through. God doesn't call us to hide our issues. He doesn't want us to push them down, compacting them into our hearts. He is not preoccupied with how we appear to others. God does not look at our outward appearance as man does (1 Sam. 16:7). He looks at our hearts with kindness. We are equipped with emotions, not bogged down by their presence.

What if we approach our sin with curiosity, rather than judgment? In a way, it serves a function. This is not meant to justify the presence of sin, but to help us understand it better. Yes, we hate the sin and love the sinner. But that's just it. How can we love the sinner? We do this by recognizing that we are human and flawed. Yes, a new creation. But one that still exists in a world surrounded by choices, to sin or not to sin. That is the question. My sin and shame *usually* point to a vulnerable place in my life. A place where I feel self-conscious, unfulfilled, or have unresolved issues. There is a God-shaped hole that I have attempted to fill with something else, leaving me never fully feeling satisfied. When we hate the sin AND the sinner, we close the door to understanding what is happening in the heart.

I have found that approaching these parts of myself—the sin-filled, shame-drenched parts and pieces—that it disengages my aversion to them. I am acknowledging my humanity and embracing humility. Several counseling models use some version of "parts work" to discern what we have buried beneath pain and trauma. The idea is to personify something that we carry with us in order to understand it more. We ask questions and allow our minds to respond naturally. When it comes to sin and shame, we disarm the defense mechanisms that prevent us from understanding the hurt beneath. It would be best to walk through this process with a professional counselor in trauma cases because the wounds require more care.

Take a moment and imagine approaching sin or shame in your life. Say to it, "I see you. I know you're hiding because it's too painful for anyone to know about you. Why are you here? What brought you here?" I'm looking for the roots, so I know where to start digging. *It will require removal.* While I am gentle in my approach, I know that sin is not beneficial. It is holding some part of me hostage.

Once I understand what led me to justify the presence of sin, I can confess it to God and ask for His forgiveness. He is so faithful to reveal the desire that is hidden behind it. The sin is unmasked and exposed for what it is—a cheap substitute. It is often clear that I haven't entrusted this area to my Savior. I have allowed fear or anxiety to spin out of control rather than pausing in prayer and handing it to Him. I've held on so tight to something that I believed I could control. First John 1:9 (ESV) says, "If we confess our sins, he is faithful and just to forgive us our sins and to cleanse us from all unrighteousness."

A gentle approach to sin does not mean it's welcome to stay. *You're done making up a warm bed and feeding it.* It requires humility to stop justifying our sins and faith to believe that God has something better for us. I experience fulfillment when I get to know the parts of me that long for more.

This Spirit-led approach is less likely to make you feel defensive. I will warn you, it does leave you feeling very vulnerable. I recommend only using parts work to understand your choices. It is not meant to be worked through alone. If you'd like more answers or to understand trauma or abuse, please get in touch with a professional who can walk you through this. It requires training to make it safely out the other side. This model can also feel strange as you personify and talk to a part of yourself you don't like or don't want others to see. But it is so helpful in moving forward! I always say that monsters are scariest in the dark. Sometimes the monsters turn out to be just trees, according *to Taylor*.[17]

Figure 4

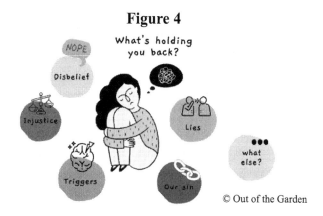

© Out of the Garden

Take it to Heart

- What has prevented you from spending time with God?

- Is there one practice from this chapter you are willing to pursue? If so, consider the steps you need to take to make it happen.

Take it to God

- Read 1 John 1:9 — Imagine introducing Jesus to the parts you explored.

- What do you imagine He would say or do?

- What healing does He offer you?

7

Transformed Mind

I am writing this chapter as Canada burns. The wildfires have caused a smoky haze to descend upon our midwestern home. The campfire smell is a constant reminder that not far from us, drought has caused the flames to blaze across more than 29,000 miles and counting. It's hard to imagine the dismay our northern neighbors are experiencing.

Do you recall how fondly I spoke of monitoring screen time? Between moving into our new home, isolating during the pandemic, rebuilding our weakened immune systems, and now this, our kids will most likely credit their tablets for teaching them everything they know. *I know. We're working on it.* Our poor air quality provided yet another reason for my kids to stay inside and entertain themselves. After a few rounds of racing cars and playing wiffle ball, we agreed to a movie.

My middle guy loves "The Lorax," especially the song, "How Ba-a-a-ad Can I Be?" The cotton candy-looking trees in the movie made me wonder if they were based on real trees or if they had some symbolic meaning. I was interested to discover that they resemble the Monterey Cypress, native to California, which is serotinous. This means they only disperse their seeds in extreme heat or *fire*. They begin the process of new life in the midst of destruction. These seeds disseminate and start again in the lush ashes of a fallen forest. My mind quickly drifts to Canada, knowing that life will slowly return there, as well. The Lorax concludes with a parade of life returning to restore the land and a Dr. Seuss quote, "Unless someone like you cares a whole awful lot, nothing is going to get better. It's not."[18]

Changing the way we think is easier said than done. It can feel like pushing a rock uphill, upstream, and in a windstorm. It would be so much easier to go with the flow. We have grown accustomed to the patterns that have formed over time. We prefer homeostasis, which means we would rather remain right where we are. We will choose discomfort in familiarity over the possibility that we could improve our circumstances. We do this because of the unknown. *What if it doesn't work?* This overbearing question keeps us small, inactive, and not achieving our goals.

In order to change the way we think, we must commit to making *one small change*. One step out of turn, one move away from the cycle. Deviating by even an inch of the norm gives us the confidence we need to revise our lives. These patterns gain momentum over time and appear unstoppable.

They often include misinterpreted actions and reactions. A symphony of expectations quietly plays on.

Neuroscientists have studied the brain and our ability to change how we think or do things, which is known as neuroplasticity. Dr. Caroline Leaf, a renowned communication pathologist and neuroscientist, has committed her research to help others comprehend brain function. She asserts that our thoughts appear like physical trees in our brains. More specifically, these neurons develop pathways that resemble a tree line that physically occupies space in our minds. In her book, *Cleaning Up the Mental Mess,* Dr. Leaf suggests the steps needed to "uproot" and change these thoughts.[19] For a detailed description, I highly recommend this book or any of her resources.

Our Spiritual House
When we began the process of having our home built, the foundation was the most important factor. Naturally, we wanted to avoid having a flooded basement or instability in the structure. I learned that the foundation does more than hold the house up. It also insulates the home, resists movement, and prevents moisture and infestation. A solid foundation is built to last forever.

We recently had a storm system blow through with a tornado warning. We raced to the basement as the wind became louder, taking out a tree and powerline. I rushed past my laptop to grab bottles of water and nearly grabbed it. I had hoped to submit this manuscript over the upcoming weekend. If a tornado hit, I could lose the whole thing. I thought to myself, "If this is an idol, I'll have to let it go."

I prayed for safety, knowing that we could experience some damage. I know that God's shelter is not a bubble—as Christ followers, we still face hard things. He shelters the mind with hope that extends beyond the physical. He provides eternal rescue because, in His infinite knowledge, He is aware of how small this life is in comparison to eternity.

In the quiet remains of the power outage, our idols were revealed. We really enjoy having power—air conditioning, Internet, and snacks from the fridge. *Please excuse me while I adjust—my privilege is showing.* At the same time, the aerator was not functioning and the heat bulb went cold, which exposed our koi and baby chicks to possible harm. I would love to say that at this point, we worked together as a team and made incredible memories by candlelight. *I wish we had that much chill.*

Instead, our methods of survival clashed and the communication towers came down. In our tired frustration, we became reactive. We worked through it and as the power returned, this verse from Ephesians 3:16 (NIV) popped up on my screen: "I pray that out of His glorious riches He may strengthen you with **power** through His Spirit in your inner being" (bold emphasis mine). The verse reminded me of His power as ours returned. *I see you, Lord.* We'd placed our attention on the wrong kind of power. While my foundation is built on Christ, the rest of the house could use repair.

In Matthew 7:24-27, Jesus introduces two men who built their homes on rock and sand. The wise man who built his home on rock withstood the rain and wind. The foolish man watched his house on the sand crumble. When we establish Christ as the foundation of our lives, we are unmovable and unshakable. Now imagine your spiritual house. We want to preserve the foundation, structure, contents, and protection from the elements. We are going to use Romans 12:2 as our guide. This verse tells us, "Do not conform to the pattern of this world, but be transformed by the renewing of your mind. Then you will be able to test and approve what God's will is—his good, pleasing and perfect will." When we take this verse, line by line, it is consistent and paramount to changing how we think. This verse provides the building blocks to shape what I'd like to call the Romans 12:2 House. It represents our spiritual transformation as we are built up in Christ. (See Figure 5)

Figure 5

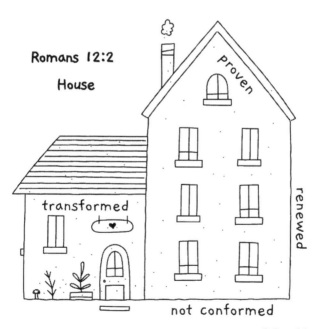

© Out of the Garden

Not Conformed

Romans 12:2 gets right to the point—and I'm here for it. First of all, God loves the world. He sky-wrote it in a banner when He offered us His Son. First John 2:16 describes worldly desires as the lust of the flesh, lust of the eyes, and pride of life. Could your damaging thoughts be characterized by any of these three? Our values change when we aim to gain success, beauty, fortune, or fame. We have our eyes on the prize, and with minor adjustments over time, we've changed where we are willing to draw the line. Pin-point intrusive thoughts and acknowledge that they are no longer working. Not conforming to the world is the foundation of our faith. Our job is to look ourselves in the eye and say *I will not allow that thought to live here anymore.*

Be Transformed

From a biblical perspective, our minds are transformed when we take a thought captive and make it obedient to Christ (2 Cor. 10:5). We take it into isolation and seek to understand how it became influential to us. Psalm 139:23, 24 formats a prayer that invites God to search our hearts and recognize what we need to lay before Him. A renewed mind replaces negative, damaging thoughts with those that glorify God. He offers the freedom to choose what fits and the discipline to know when it doesn't. Transformation requires the basic care of our hearts and minds. We replace what no longer works, throw fresh paint on the walls, and tidy up the joint—even the nooks and crannies. We replace the old with the new. The transformed mind is committed to regular upkeep.

Renewed

A renewed mind has the power to reframe thoughts as they arise. Hitting the refresh button is a life-long process that requires practice to become a habit—and will still require effort. Restoration is evident when people regulate emotions and respond appropriately in social situations. While negative thoughts still exist, they are no longer calling the shots. Transforming our lives requires the courage to restore the broken places. We fear removing our present from the shadows of the past. It is common to avoid them because they remind us of a time when we lacked control or experienced pain.

You may be walking through the shattered areas of your life right now. Surrounded by shards of glass and broken treasures, you're still determining your next step. The lack of control and present pain consume your days because you haven't made it across to the other side. You are not viewing this through the rearview mirror—it is now and you are asking yourself what to do next.

Our circumstances do not define our story. We are encouraged by Romans 8:38, 39 (ESV), "For I am sure that neither death nor life, nor angels nor rulers, nor things present nor things to come, nor powers, nor height nor depth, nor anything else in all creation, will be able to separate us from the love of God in Christ Jesus our Lord." *Nothing can separate us from God's love.*

What are the things that feel as though they are separating you from God's love? I think of the man-made rules that emphasize in our fallenness—addiction, adultery, divorce, tattoos, piercings, race, sexuality, gender, abuse, neglect, etc. We wear them on our skin and in our hearts. *God could not love me in this.* This verse is repetitive and thorough as it concludes that there is nothing on this earth that can separate us from God's redeeming love. He knows our deepest longings and desires—He understands these places that feel confusing in our culture. Who am I to say that anyone cannot be loved and restored by His power?

I would like you to take these verses and fill in the blanks with the things you believe are not forgiven. Claim the power of the cross by submitting each one to Christ.

For I am sure that neither _____, nor _____, nor _____, nor _____, nor _____, nor _____, nor _____, nor _____, nor _____, nor _____ anything else in all creation, will be able to separate us from the love of God in Christ Jesus our Lord.

A transformed mind recognizes negative patterns and replaces them with Truth. We utilize boundaries and wise guidance to make the best decisions. A strong mind frames the spiritual house, holding it all together. Just as a home is layered with siding, insulation, and solid framing, our minds are pieced together with experiences and past successes or failures. Revitalization occurs when we take it one step further and prepare for circumstances that might cause us to slide into old thought patterns. It helps to visualize how we would respond in those moments. We want our brains to memorize these ideas by storing them all over. The more we engage our minds, the more we will experience transformation.

Proven

Our renewal is evident in the way our thoughts and actions become more proactive and less reactive. By using the Word of God to shape our identity, we are able to combat negative thoughts and ideas. We recognize the Shepherd's voice. In a sense, the brain can only "eat" what we are "feeding" it. Once we stop feasting on unhelpful thoughts, we'll gain the confidence to continue this life-changing habit. We may not *eliminate* these thoughts, but we learn to not feel powerless in their presence. It's an incredible realization when we find that some thoughts can be ignored.

The proven mind exhibits new patterns in thoughts and behavior. This evidence includes continually uprooting negative thoughts and ideas, replacing them with Truth, and looking for ways to prevent future relapse. Considering the things we put in our minds reminded me of my experience with the virtual reality game *Richie's Plank Experience*.[20] I am not a fan of heights, but I donned the headset and gave it a go. In this game, I stepped into an elevator, patiently waited as it carried me to the top story of a skyscraper, and stepped out on a plank that overlooked a city. My heart began to race when I looked down. The sights and sounds told my body I could fall, even though I was actually standing in my living room. The first time I jumped or fell off the plank, my heart raced, and my body braced for impact. My brain was so confused. I couldn't believe how intensely my body reacted to this video game.

Like any logical human, I continued doing this until I was completely desensitized to the physiological response. It worked! While my brain still responded to what it was seeing, it sent a weaker signal to the rest of my body, letting it know I would be okay. I found that with repeated exposure, I was no longer limited to what I saw. My experience outweighed what my mind thought to be true.

In the same way, faith requires us to look beyond what we can see. Evidence of a renewed mind will ultimately point toward glorifying God. Colossians 3:2 states this beautifully, claiming that our minds are set on things above, no longer earthly things. Matthew 6:21 points to our treasure to locate our hearts because they are never far behind. When we emphasize the importance of the physical world, we define ourselves by what we see. We experience restoration when our motive shifts from meeting our demands to fulfilling His plans. A proven faith acts as a roof to the spiritual house, weathering storms and protecting from the elements.

Take it to Heart

- How have you experienced a transformed mind?

- What is one small change you can commit to making in your life?

- What changes would you like to see in your life five years from now (as a result of changing the way you think)?

Take it to God

- Read Romans 12:2 — Pray about the areas in your life that you have conformed to the world.

- Pray for wisdom to understand the areas you have not submitted or continue to experience difficulty. What are some of the distorted beliefs you hold?

- Meditate on new thoughts that will be helpful and true.

8

The Brain on Change

I'm a proud member of the D.A.R.E. generation. If you know what this means, then you likely have taken a firm stand against the war on skinny jeans and still rock a side part. *Maybe you don't and I stand alone.* For those of us who watched TV with commercials—one shared TV with scheduled programming—you may recall the egg being fried in a pan as we were told that "This was your brain on drugs."[21] The war on drugs was in full effect and D.A.R.E. visited our schools and TV to tell us, "Just say no." *Thank you for this helpful tip.*

The message and methods of this program had a few flaws. Our minds are more complex than fragile yolks. While the damage caused by drug use can be pervasive, it is not always permanent. Many parents who had dabbled in recreational drug use during the '60s still had their wits about them. This disempowered the message we'd received and left us with many questions. An epidemic of drug use continues today, despite the valiant efforts of this program.

The Brain on Change
If you're able to switch gears with me, I'd like to leave behind the brain on drugs and focus on the brain on change. As I thought about the renewal of our minds, I imagined the various regions of our brains getting involved. It is as though they are online and ready for action. Each part responds to the environment in a different way. As I studied the brain, it occurred to me that coping skills can be stored in different regions. This dynamic approach fully equips us to make and maintain change. I've illustrated this concept in Figure 6, "The Brain on Change."

Figure 6

© Out of the Garden

Each lobe performs a different function to promote healthy functioning:

- The frontal lobe is ignited by planning, using our judgment, and when concentrating.[22] This part of the brain, which sits behind our forehead, is used in this process of thought formation. We replace unhelpful beliefs with new thoughts in this region.

- The parietal lobes, near the center of your brain, interpret the environment and your body by engaging the senses.[23] A heightened response usually causes us to react. It's essential to pause and consider what we are feeling. If we are not in a threatening situation, we can scan our environment for other sensory responses. What can you taste or touch in your current environment?

  The brain analyzes the five senses in different parts, and using them makes us feel grounded in the present moment. Emotional responses are like hot air balloons, making us feel like we are floating away with them. Our senses keep our feet on the ground. They remind us where we are in the present. The Bible notes the importance of our senses. In Psalm 34:8, David said to taste and see that the Lord is good. This psalm of praise is a reminder that God protected David, who was faithful and true.

- The occipital lobe is responsible for processing what we see. We utilize this region to recognize faces, store memories, and understand depth and color. The visual neurons housed here are activated by what we see and even physical trauma, such as a bump to the head or even a concussion, which causes us to "see stars." This region is also where memories are stored. When our interpretation is that something is off, we are unsafe, or we need to get out of a situation, our body begins responding to the signal.[24] We seek to understand this interpretation further when we ask ourselves, "What do I see?".

To experience God's transformation in our mind, we fix our eyes on Jesus. Hebrews 12:2 (NIV) says, "Fixing our eyes on Jesus, the pioneer and perfecter of faith. For the joy set before Him, He endured the cross, scorning its shame, and sat down at the right hand of the throne of God." This verse comforted me because the truth can be ugly. *I messed up. That person let me down. I don't have what I need. How can I fix this? What should I do next?* Let's call this "little t" truth. It is limited to our circumstances. Sometimes, we misperceive things and allow that to influence the way we think about ourselves or others.

In these moments, we need to adjust our vision. The "big T" Truth has not changed. God has not abandoned us. Just like an author would not publish a book half-written, He is not giving up on us mid-chapter. James MacDonald stated: "God's love is not a pampering love. God's love is a perfecting love. God does not get up every day trying to figure out how He can plant a bigger smile on your face. God is in the process of growing and changing us. His love is a transforming love."[25] When the odds *appear* to be against us, we can think about what we *know* to be true. Even if it is as simple as the heart beating in your chest, rest in the reality that He is not done yet.

- The brainstem sends signals from the brain to the rest of the body. It is vital to our survival, as it controls our breathing, heart rate, blood pressure, consciousness, and sleep. This bridge between the mind and body requires little upkeep for optimal transportation. It is simply part of our functioning. When we feel anxious, we can engage this part of our mind with deep breathing, allowing our racing heart to return to normal. We invite this bridge, swaying wildly in the wind of our uncertainty, to be stilled by what it does best: *slow down and breathe.* Our minds are easily influenced but also can be regulated. Psalm 3:5 (NIV) says, "I lie down and sleep; I wake again, because the Lord sustains me." God knows the number of days in our lives. There is nothing we can do to change that. Sometimes our gratitude rests only in the fact that we woke up this morning. *It's a good start.*

- The cerebellum coordinates movement and makes us aware of a change in posture and how we carry ourselves. Specific thoughts may cause us to hunch over, almost symbolic of how we draw into ourselves. Scripture suggests that our body mirrors what we are working through. Whether burdened by sin or expressing gratitude, we might find ourselves on our knees in humble confession or raising our hands to worship God. We mirror our circumstances by folding in on ourselves or extending our bodies. Seeking His presence and expressing gratitude are crucial to thought renewal.

- The temporal lobe interprets what we see and hear in the world around us. There is one near the ears on either side of the head. This part of the brain interprets facial expressions, language, and emotions in other people. It also aids in storing memories. Reframing our thoughts requires us to discern the difference between what is happening and what we believe is happening in our social encounters. We can misinterpret others' behavior when we "mind-read" or make assumptions. In 2 Timothy 1:7 (NIV), we are told, "For the Spirit God gave us does not make us timid, but gives us power, love and self-discipline." The Holy Spirit promotes a healthy thought life. We have access to resources beyond our strength and ability. God designed our minds to hold new information and replace useless patterns.

- The hippocampus and amygdala reside in the temporal lobes. They are reactive to one another, and used to keep us safe at a moment's notice. Lessons learned and memories earned get tucked away here. Past negative experiences do make it all a bit fuzzy. I imagine our ready-for-action amygdala donning boxing gloves and pushing our logical prefrontal cortex out of the way. *There is a coup afoot.* The amygdala goes into fight or flight, no longer listening to reason. This response determines whether it should fight the problem or flee the scene. We are unable to fully connect when our minds are focused on survival.

When experiencing fight or flight, we will recall times we have felt this way before. While the circumstances have changed, our body responds as though it is the same. The message being sent to our body is that we must decide. *And fast.* In a split second, before we have time to think about it, our mind springs into action and exerts or reserves energy to get through the perceived threat. The speed of our response is both crucial and alarming. It can feel like we are out of control and unable to change how we respond. What is meant for survival sometimes distorts how we see our current situation. The result is an over-exerted nervous system that requires respite. The amygdala responds with fight or flight based on what has happened in the past. We can soothe the amygdala with mindful breaths and meditation. The hippocampus is able to reset and store the memory of current safety. Over time, these new experiences will allow this dynamic duo to chill out.

Rather than worrying about "what if," we can shift our minds to "what is." Philippians 4:4-9 (NIV) tells us to take the following steps:

- Rejoice in the Lord always. *Seriously, rejoice.*
- Be outwardly gentle
- Do not be anxious about anything
- Pray to God for everything
- His response will be unfailing, unfathomable peace
- So stop worrying about "what if." Focus on whatever is:
- True, noble, right, pure, lovely, admirable, excellent, praiseworthy. Think about these things.

A helpful view of the renewed mind is found in the book, "Finding God in the Waves." Christian author, Mike McHargue, shares his experience as a Christian, then atheist, and once again believer. He credits science for his return to faith. He says,

> "The Loving God affects the brain in ways that are remarkably different from the Angry God. People who focus on God's love develop thicker, richer gray matter in their prefrontal cortex and anterior cingulate cortex. This development offers them better focus, concentration, compassion, and empathy. They have lower stress levels and lower blood pressure, and it's easier for them to forgive themselves and others. Over time, they even show less activity in the amygdala. Even more, people who believe that God is loving will eventually develop a characteristic asymmetry in the activity of their thalamus. When that happens, God's love becomes implanted in their sense of identity, and they begin to see the world as being basically safe. This not only allows the believer to experience peace —it also elevates her capacity to take risks for the sake of others. For those who know the Loving God, the risk of being hurt in relationships is less important, because God's love will transcend that hurt."[26]

A renewed mind is brought to life by Our Great Rescuer. His love is practically and unmatchably transformative. Just as God's Word sinks in between muscle and marrow, His love stills the wildest storms in our minds. We may not know the entry point, but evidence of His peace fills us in exceptional ways. A restored mind is not dulled by submission but rather brought to new life and purpose.

Take it to Heart

- What are your current coping skills? Is there a negative skill that needs to be replaced?

- How is this understanding of the brain helpful to you?

- What is one new coping skill you can use to support a healthier way of thinking?

Take it to God

- Read Philippians 4:4-9. Replace negative thoughts and beliefs with these verses. It may be helpful to write this verse out so that you become familiar with the list.

- Pray for wisdom in replacing your negative thoughts. Invite the Holy Spirit to help you change.

9

The Four C's

Navigating the Four C's
Welcome to the final chapters of our tour. We have visited the Abundant Life while it is under construction. All of you had a sneak peek at The Brain on Change, the future site, and newest location of the Transformed Mind. We hope your visit to Intentional Rest is always refreshing as you enjoy our accommodations and services. We apologize for the turbulence as we passed through What's Holding You Back? We do hope you enjoyed the complimentary refreshments during your stay. We are now entering The Four C's, so please keep your arms in at all times, and don't forget to tip your cocktail waitress.

I have clearly never been on a cruise, but I imagine they do want you to keep your arms and the rest of you securely in and on the ship at all times. My travel plans have recently been problematic—canceled planes, missed trains, and over-booked automobiles. These are the moments when push comes to shove. We must make decisions on the spot as the people around us are also scrambling to reach their destination. We watch as other people's frantic expectations trample over our best-laid plans. Our opposing ideas become chaos when resources are limited.

Compare l Compete l Complain l Conflict

Compare
Comparison is not innately problematic. When comparison is appropriately used, we establish personal goals with boundaries. The line between *us* and *them* is clear, recognizing individual strengths and possibilities. We celebrate other people's achievements. Consider a comparison chart you might view before buying a product. It relays a checklist of qualities that are not good or bad; they just *are*. The information is not the problem, but it is designed to subtly coax us into believing the added qualities will improve our experience. *For a small additional cost, you can have it all.*

We frequently use comparisons to measure ourselves against others based on a better than/worse than rating system. As a result, we may lack compassion or feel inadequate. *You snooze, you lose.* Just as keeping a tally of rights and wrongs is not helpful, grading our worth based on those around us is damaging. While it is driven by insecurity, a comparison might cause us to behave like we are better than others.

Ephesians 4:18, 19 describes this way of thinking as darkened, separated, and greedy. A hardened heart seeks to be satisfied by physical pleasure. Ultimately, it is rooted in uncertainty. We look to the people and places around us to make sense of our experiences. We have some questions driving us to focus on the people around us. *How do other people do it? How could I make this better? How can I be better?* If we aren't careful, we view ourselves negatively—or we feel better about ourselves and quickly judge the other person.

Compete
When we compare, we often compete. We are less likely to be generous when we are competing with others. A social tug-of-war may appear anywhere from a workplace promotion to a "friendly" neighborhood rivalry. *I consider the PTA and shudder.* Our PTA president is a rockstar, but I've heard stories of these groups that would keep you up at night. Invisible trophies create winners and losers, which might lead to us celebrating our victories over others. We secretly love when someone is less than perfect. We feel like losers in light of someone else's success. Community and connection are often disrupted by the belief that I *deserve* this. I am *better* at this. I *should* be recognized. Rather than experiencing meaningful relationships with depth and authenticity, we are left to interact with others who desire to "win" as well.

Competition is driven by how we want to be seen by others. Winning is a social accomplishment, so we contend with people pursuing similar goals and desired roles. In most cases, we want to stand out for the *right reasons*. We want to be memorable. Our lives are made fuller by getting involved, but we aren't the only ones who are thinking this.

Competition could be healthy when our motives align with our values—a title next to our name points to our strengths and abilities. We may have acquired the training or expertise to be an excellent candidate to be considered. The world needs high achievers who aren't afraid to put in some elbow grease and get things done. Success is earned—ideally, it won't leave others borrowed and bruised.

Complaints
Cue the complaints. If we believe there is a discrepancy or a chance we will be left out, fall behind, or not feel valued, we are already focused on the negative! We believe our circumstances will stay the same. We're full of excuses for why we have not reached our goals. We feel relief when we vent because it *seems* like we're addressing the issue. But that's all we're doing, letting out hot air. And do you know what hot air does? *It spoils things.*

Complaining pours out of our expectations for others. Sometimes they are unrealistic or unspoken, but we verbalize judgments about how they are showing up in the world. We *can't believe they would* this, and *I would do* that. Complaining is often the result of disappointment and discouragement. Our feelings are often justified, but the responses are not. When we complain, we want the other person to care about our experience enough to change what they are doing. Unfortunately, accusations and criticisms rarely get the response we desire. Anger is not the problem—the response is.

Conflict
Complaining leads to conflict. I believe that honesty is the best policy. I really do. However, a *how*, a *why*, and a perfectly timed *when* is also important. Appropriately handling conflict

is a master's class in human communication, and few of us have completed the course. Our motive may be to resolve an issue, but a negative mindset complicates the message. Heck, a positive frame of mind sometimes goes over poorly.

Conflict often creates distance in relationships. We may shy away from being honest with others because we fear damaging the relationship. We want to remain close, even if it is strenuous. We avoid accountability at the risk of being labeled as dramatic or judgmental. We want to see change and resolution. Still, when the pattern has moved from comparing to competition to complaining, we need to be in the right headspace to handle conflict appropriately.

Many people are unsure of how to resolve issues in their relationships. We often leave an argument feeling frustrated and unclear of what will happen next. It can be awkward, so we may distance ourselves from one another. Past experiences might indicate that someone is not emotionally equipped to respond appropriately to our concerns.

Replacing the 4 C's
During the Han Dynasty, the Four Seas represented bodies of water that surrounded ancient China. Confucius, a wise teacher who promoted unity and ethical living, shared proverbs that are still used today. In a conversation about virtue, he said, "Let the superior man never fail reverentially to order his own conduct, and let him be respectful to others and observant of propriety:-then all within the four seas will be his brothers."[27] *I feel like a wise, ancient sensei.* While the Four Seas marked their borders, the saying was meant to unite all of humanity, no matter the culture or race.

As we dive into the Four C's (pun intended), we can use these words as our guide. We exemplify Christ when we treat others with dignity. However, when we are focused on our deficits, our goals become self-seeking. We want to soothe the discomfort brought on by these encounters. A scarcity mindset turns our gaze inward. The actual issue is hidden under jealousy, envy, disappointment, anger, regret, etc. It's found in what we tell ourselves about ourselves and the other people involved. If our choices leave us feeling insecure, depleted, and defeated, are we genuinely experiencing freedom?

True freedom is the result of intentional living. Good vibes and happy thoughts might get you through the day, but a heart pumping with gratitude and purpose will get you through the long night. Ephesians 4:17 tells us to leave behind futile thinking. Our obedience results in a healthier mind. We are able to displace the negative habits of the four C's and replace them with the following:

Curiosity l Collaborate l Celebrate l Communicate

Curiosity
If comparing is rooted in insecurity, we can replace it with curiosity. *What am I drawn to? Is this important to me? Is this a good fit for me?* Instead of feeling shame for the more than/less than results, we look at our goals and see if this is for us. Take your strengths and areas of improvement into account. Are you equipped for this? The answer may be *no, but I can work at it.* Or, it may be, *no, and I'm not sure I ever will be.* It may even be, *yes, but this isn't important to me.* By accepting what is possible and realistic, we can set attainable goals.

Curiosity is helpful when I'm taking on new things. In my practice, I am fascinated by new approaches to therapy. Some require additional training or certification. I have to weigh the options and determine if this is a style I can adopt or am committed to learning more about. Not surprisingly, I do this with parenting hacks, marriage menders, and artistic outlets. I'm a consumer at heart, so I want to believe this *simple trick* will change our lives. Rather than comparing what I am doing to others, I often need to go this added step to consider if I have the time or resources to incorporate this new thing into my life. Even if it appears to do wonders for your marriage and family, it may not fit in my world.

Ephesians 4:1-13 tells us that Christ equipped different types of people to serve in unique ways to build up the body of believers. We are called to unity, which requires humility, gentleness, patience, and love. I believe God is able to draw anyone from any walk of life to Him. For that reason, I do my best to express curiosity toward others and not judge what I don't understand. I want my eyes to be open if and when He puts off the old and replaces it with the new (Eph. 4:20-24).

Collaborate
We replace competing with collaborating. How can we work together to achieve our goals without stepping over each other? How can we set boundaries and clearly defined roles? How can we value each other more? Our ability to work well with others exhibits our character.

Working together displays maturity and restores a sound mind. Ephesians 4:15-16 (NIV) says, "Instead, speaking the Truth in love, we will grow to become in every respect the mature body of him who is the head, that is, Christ. From Him the whole body, joined and held together by every supporting ligament, grows and builds itself up in love, as each part does its work." Even obedience in our speech can draw us closer to Christ. Through Him, we have different purposes within one body. He makes it all work together.

The verses leading up to this state that we must equip people to build the church (v. 12) and be unified (v. 13). Sometimes, this requires facing difficult conversations or changing our approach. A curious mind asks well-timed questions. When we are open to new ideas, we are open to fresh ways of doing things. Collaboration is based on the practice, not the end result. You are developing character, not success. Collaboration does not guarantee a favorable outcome. You can only control the way you present yourself to the world.

Collaborating is not about getting what you want to feel good about yourself. It's not about being the best. You may *not* be the best here. It's all about being the kind of person who does not become successful by climbing on the backs of others. I picture hoisting one another up, like interlacing your fingers and assuring a friend you can lift them. We can lift others up or hold them back. Which one do you want to be known for?

While there is a need for cooperation, collaboration is also about boundaries. We are working toward the same goal, but we have different roles. *I will do this; you will do that.* Assigning roles often reveals the other person's motives and allows you to manage your expectations. Setting clear guidelines is the foundation of building something successful together.

Celebrate

Complaining is the result of unmet expectations. Many times they are valid concerns. Sometimes our complaints are the exhausted outcry for fair treatment, respect, and commitment from others. The other person may ignore our gentle approach—we may find ourselves all out of grace at the moment.

The problem with these negative feelings is that they do not keep to themselves. A heart full of complaints suddenly sees the bad in other things. Examples of wrongdoings and mistreatment suddenly surround us. It feels unfair, and we feel entitled to a change.

The most significant way to combat negativity in our lives is with gratitude. We shift our complaints to celebrations. As Christ followers, we've been given victory over the temporary. We can fully experience hardships without allowing them to define us. *I feel broken by this, but I am not broken.* We are not pretending everything is hunky dory—we are choosing to rise above. Ephesians 4:29 tells us to build each other up, not tear each other down with our words.

Ephesians 4:30-32 tells us how to respond: "And do not grieve the Holy Spirit of God, with whom you were sealed for the day of redemption. Get rid of all bitterness, rage and anger, brawling and slander, along with every form of malice. Be kind and compassionate to one another, forgiving each other, just as in Christ God forgave you." Ideally, our words would not make the Holy Spirit wince as we say them. Our redemption may be signed, sealed, and delivered, but God also wants others to receive it.

Our bitter, angry hearts are behind the unkind things we say. When we embrace the forgiveness we have received, we can wholeheartedly offer it to those who have hurt us. Not to give them access to us or allow for more damage. But to release both of us of a burden we no longer have to carry.

Communicate
Conflict is inevitable, but we can use it to communicate. Even as we are doing our best to work together, we disagree. Imagine traveling through life with baggage that contains life experiences, love, pain, joy, and suffering. No matter how much we may care for another person, that baggage travels with us. Their affection does not empty the bag. We face storms, make mistakes, and sometimes hurt each other along the way. It's impossible to avoid. We are responsible for managing our emotions and communicating respectfully. We are not responsible for *eliminating* negative experiences. It's part of being human. When we have realistic standards, we can accept others more graciously.

Respectful communication involves taking responsibility for our part, expressing our feelings about the situation, and being clear about what we want or need. It is not blaming, criticizing, attacking character, labeling, name-calling, or assuming what the other person is thinking. *Two wrongs don't make a right.* Our anger does not justify a disrespectful response. Ephesians 4:26, 27 (NIV) warns us, "'In your anger, do no sin:' Do not let the sun go down while you are still angry, and do not give the devil a foothold." Psalm 4:4, 5 tells us to search our hearts and be silent while trusting in the Lord.

Rationalizing that the other person deserves this treatment actually delays the response we are hoping for. They might become defensive, not wanting to engage in an unhealthy communication pattern. The conversation now shifts from the original issue to creating new boundaries about the way it was brought up. Neither person feels satisfied in the wake of a verbal attack.

We interpret other people's words and body language while they are speaking. We may question the motive behind the comment. Our response is aggressive when we assume our interpretation is correct and react to the other person negatively. A passive-aggressive response is indirect, often communicated through negative comments and closed-off body language. An assertive response wants to communicate clearly by asking questions and sharing how it feels to be on the other side of these words.

One way to respond assertively would be to ask, "What did you mean by that?" In closer relationships that allow open communication, we can share our interpretation and how the encounter made us feel. Healthy conflict aims to *make things right* with the other person—*not to prove that we are right*. It is far more inclusive to hear both sides, take responsibility for our feelings, words, and actions, and decide what each person needs to move forward.

Some conflict is one-sided and unwarranted. We have not provoked the issue or caused a problem. The goal may not be reconciliation or resolution. Discern what God has for us when we release it to Him, but even then, we do not receive quick, easy answers. Relationships with a pattern of unhealthy and damaging interactions often require firm boundaries. Many people struggle with this because it's difficult to tell others "no," and it is often not well-received. Boundaries are limits—most people do not celebrate them. Most people would rather ignore a problem than risk disconnection from the person they are struggling with.

Whatever the issue, it's important to ask yourself what you hope to get out of a difficult conversation. What's your motive? What are you hoping the outcome will be? How will you know this issue is resolved? What are you committed to doing differently? Ultimately, we can only control our own behavior.

Live Loved
Consider the Four C's as you engage with other people. Figure 7 provides a visual reminder of how we can replace our negative habits with those that are healthy and will benefit our relationships. God's Word offers us freedom from scarcity thinking. We are imperfect, but God shows unconditional love. Jesus shifted the focus from our sins to His redemption in His life, death, and resurrection on our behalf. *On our behalf.* How easily we forget what Jesus did for us when we magnify the problems in our lives. In the face of many challenges, we can think intentionally about living loved and view people through that same lens.

Figure 7

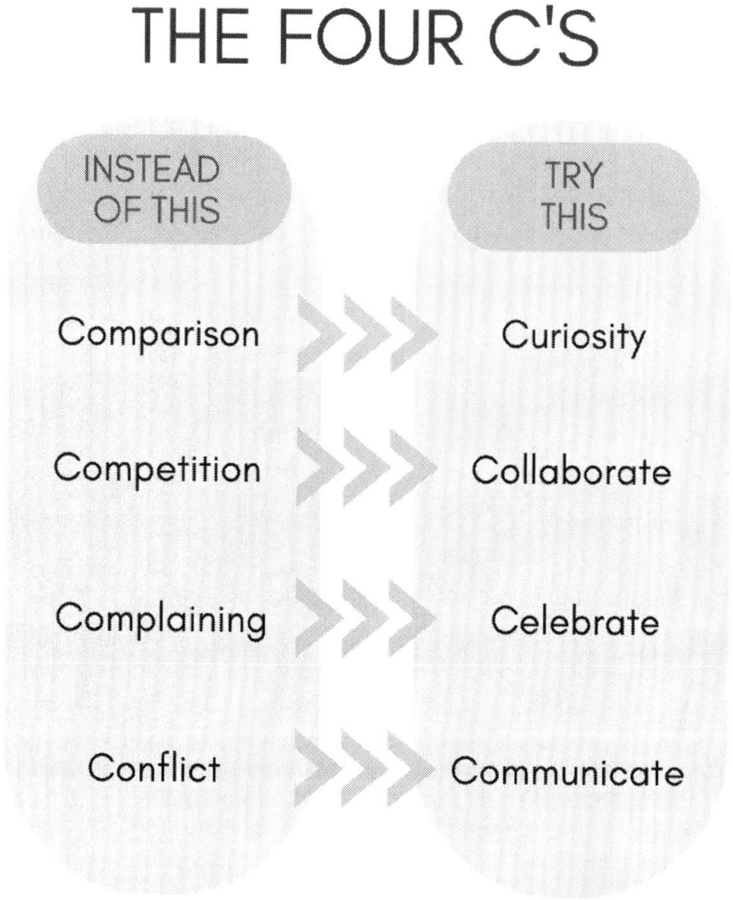

THE FOUR C'S

INSTEAD OF THIS		TRY THIS
Comparison	>>>	Curiosity
Competition	>>>	Collaborate
Complaining	>>>	Celebrate
Conflict	>>>	Communicate

© Out of the Garden

Take it to Heart

- Where have you experienced the Four C's in your life? Can you think of examples?

- Have you experienced any consequences as a result of this way of thinking?

- What are some of the changes you would like to see in your relationships?

- How can you replace the Four C's as you relate to others? If helpful, think of specific examples.

Take it to God

- Read Ephesians 4 — How do these verses align with our response to the four C's?

- Imagine the body of Christ, made up of fellow believers. Imagine each person's purpose. Ask God to bless their ministry.

- Pray for the strength to build a legacy of love that honors Christ.

10

Women in the Word

Jesus came to restore lives to the Father. In many ways, He restored the narrative for women. In John 4:4-26, Jesus first revealed His identity to the woman at the well when He asked her for water. Other Jewish men would have despised her for being Samaritan and female, but Jesus saw her. He knew her story. She was a Samaritan woman who had five husbands and at least one lover (that we know of). Her race, gender, and array of sexual partners made her untouchable. In verse twenty-six, Jesus reveals His identity as the Messiah to her. From that day forward, what Jewish people thought of her would not have mattered. Her people could have said, "Those people hate us," and she could have countered it with, "Not their King. He saw me. *He made me worthy*."

This story is a beautiful reflection of a time when another woman, at another well, cried out to God, and He responded. In

Genesis 16:1-14 we meet Hagar, Sarah's mistress, who was pregnant with Abraham's son. In her seemingly stunted fertility, Sarah became jealous and mistreated Hagar. An angel of the Lord found Hagar and told her to return (v. 7). He informed her that her descendants would be innumerable. He offered her a family for generations to come.

This gracious glimpse of what would be gave Hagar the courage to face Abraham and Sarah, but first, she acknowledged the Lord in Genesis 16:13 (NIV) by saying, "You are the God who sees me," for she said, "I have now seen the One who sees me." *A woman was the first person in the Bible to name God.* From that day forward, the well was called Beer Lahai Roi, which means W*ell of the Living One who sees me.* These women were parched, and God refreshed their lives with living water.

One of the most impactful stories I know is that of the woman who suffered from a bleeding disorder for twelve years (Mark 5:22-43). Jairus, a leader in the synagogue, pleaded with Jesus to save the man's dying daughter. The crowd pressed on, no doubt slowing down the process. Just then, Jesus stopped. He asked who touched Him. If I were Jairus, I would've been climbing out of my skin at this point—me, *them, all of us, Lord! We don't have time for this!*

The suffering woman touched Jesus' robe, fell at His feet, and trembled with fear (v. 33). *She knew He was clothed in righteousness.* Mark tells us that when she touched His garment, she was immediately healed (v. 29). This woman spent all of her life's savings visiting doctors without answers and experienced years of being rejected by society.

Jesus took it all away upon contact. In the *Encounters at the Feet of Jesus* study, Michelle pointed out that Jesus wanted to acknowledge her so she could share her testimony and no longer live in hiding. In Mark 5:34, Jesus called her daughter and said her faith had healed her. He brought her out of years of shame, isolation, and social disgrace. She is the only woman in Scripture Jesus referred to as *daughter*. A woman whose own family had likely disowned her. A woman we know by her disorder, not by name. How fitting, as He was on His way to help Jairus' daughter—Jairus, whose name was interpreted to mean "Yhwh will awaken." *And that He did.*

In the meantime, word reached Jairus that his daughter had died, and there was no sense in "bothering" the Teacher anymore (v. 53). This did not stop Jesus. He pressed on with the journey and raised the young girl from the dead. Mark 5:42 tells us that this girl was twelve years old. *Twelve years.* This girl's life measured the same amount of time as the woman's suffering. This young girl, facing womanhood and her own fertility, was in stark contrast to the woman unable to conceive for so many years. Infertility would have felt like a death sentence in a society that extensively valued childbirth. Jesus did not reverse that, but He did not make her wait any longer. Just as Jairus longed for his daughter to heal, Jesus also longed to heal His daughter. No earthly condition can remove the love of our Father. Jesus restored life specifically to meet each of their unique needs.

Jesus made a habit of showing kindness to women. He pitied a woman who had lost her only son and raised him from the dead (Luke 7:11-14). He straightened the back of the bent-over woman (Luke 13:12). Jesus healed Mary Magdalene of seven demons and allowed her to join the ministry (Mark 16:9; Luke 8:1-3). Mary showed gratitude by breaking a vase and pouring expensive perfume over Jesus' feet. We are once again reminded of what our Savior can do with a broken vessel.

The Old Testament introduces us to women who were hidden in society. They were ordinary and scandalous, preferably forgotten by people from their time. We witness the lives of the first women, no less prone to comparison, jealousy, hard feelings, and wanting more. When I think of the value God places on women, five, in particular, stand out to me.

Tamar

Judah's daughter-in-law, Tamar, was widowed and deceived by two of his sons. Desperate, she pretended to be a prostitute with Judah, keeping his seal and cord for leverage. When word got out that she was pregnant, Judah spared her when he saw his belongings, quickly piecing together that he was the father. She gave birth to his twins, continuing Judah's bloodline (Genesis 38:6-30).

Bathsheba

Bathsheba was beautiful, married, and exposed in the moonlight of her rooftop bath. Second Samuel 11:2-22 introduces her in just this light as David watches nearby. *King David.* The once shepherd boy is now king and has the world at his fingertips. David orchestrated a plan to have her for the night, which resulted in her untimely pregnancy. He elaborated on the agenda by having her husband, Uriah, return from battle to be with her.

This plan backfired when Uriah slept at the doorstep, having exhausted himself from going to war on David's behalf. David had Uriah sent to the front of the battlefield to ensure his death and wrap up the whole debacle. Bathsheba—who had no part in any of this—mourned for her husband, became David's wife, and bore him a son. She suffered the loss of a child for his sins.

Tamar
David's daughter, Tamar (2 Samuel 13), was taken against her will by her half-brother, Amnon, who had obsessed over her beauty and premeditated the assault. He hatefully discarded her afterward, no doubt riddled with guilt for what he had done. He not only robbed her of honor but blamed her for it, as well. Amnon violated her and tarnished her view of sexuality. Tamar's shame became public as her brother, Absalom, sought to avenge her. He brutally murdered Amnon, which meant that he needed to disappear. She lost her dignity and her brother. Absalom continued on a path of destruction, leaving her to grapple with shame and blame. Bloodshed and pain resulted from this violation. Tamar's story was painfully similar to that of another member of her family tree, Dinah. Jacob's daughter was also taken against her will and avenged by her brothers with bloodshed and destruction (Genesis 34). These women no doubt felt vulnerable, weak, and exposed, marked by the penalty of being a woman.

Ruth
Ruth came from an unfavorable bloodline. The Moab people were pagans that resulted from incest. Ruth witnessed the death of her father-in-law, husband, and brother-in-law. She pledged her loyalty to her grieving mother-in-law, Naomi, who told her to go on with her life. Ruth returned to Bethlehem with Naomi

and went to the field to find discarded grain for the women to eat. The land owner, Boaz, noticed the way Ruth cared for her Naomi, and he looked after her. He followed the protocol to ensure that a guardian-redeemer would see these women, but the first-in-line wanted to avoid risking his assets at the cost of marrying Ruth. In his mind, it was a risky move. Boaz quickly stepped up and married her, and the two had a son.

God restored Ruth's family tree. We see a glimpse of redemption for Tamar (Judah's daughter-in-law) as she is mentioned in Ruth 4:12. Her decision to preserve the family tree is both honored and redeemed. This decision resulted in a lineage of noble and noteworthy men and women. The Bible emphatically recognizes children as a gift from God.

Rahab
Finally, we meet Rahab in Joshua 2:1-21. Two of Joshua's spies found shelter in this known prostitute's home as the king of Jericho pursued them. She bravely denied their presence when asked to turn the Israelite spies over to the authorities. After lying that the men had headed off in one direction, she went to where she had hidden them. Rahab spoke vulnerably about the fear her people felt toward these men. She also acknowledged that God would deliver Jericho to their hands and asked them to show her kindness. They formed a truce because of her faithfulness.

Bloodline
There is something incredible about each of these stories. *All of these women came from Jesus' bloodline.* These women were deceitful, dishonest, disloyal, and disowned. They were single mothers, adulterers, and prostitutes. Modern society would tear

them apart on social media, sharing unflattering photos and marking them with disgrace. God chose imperfect women to bear life after life until Christ was finally born. The Father saw insight, beauty, courage, and loyalty. Jesus offered second chances. He used the strengths they had and did not waste their pain. Through their brokenness, we can rest and know the extent of His love.

Do you see redemption in the broken places of your story? When you look back, do you see the healing marks and fading scars? Where have you been rooted in strength and removed from mistakes? Your story is not over, my friend. Rest in truth and walk with courage. Allow your mind to be restored when you feel depleted. He knows your individual needs. God will fill your life in ways that are more than anything earthly you could hope or imagine.

Take it to Heart

- What is the significance of Jesus revealing His true identity to the woman at the well?

- What is the significance of Hagar being the first woman to name God?

- Can you relate to any of the women in these stories?

- In what ways might Jesus restore your story as a woman?

Take it to God

- Read Psalm 46:10 — Pray this verse to God, asking Him to reveal the places you need to be still.

- Seek wisdom in the places you need to trust Him.

- Praise Him for the ways He is still more powerful than our circumstances.

11

Two Worlds

As Christ followers, we live in the tension between two worlds. *Some days, it is palpable.* We have one foot on each side, telling ourselves we can do it all. This dual citizen conflicts with our ability to be fully present. Like double agents, it is difficult to know where our loyalties lie. We appear off-balanced and uncommitted.

Jesus was the first and only to know both worlds. He walked with God in perfection before entering the world. His human form likely was pierced by splinters and easily bruised long before He hung on the cross. Christ walked among people He loved and understood as they experienced life together. Jesus preserved His perfection because He knew His immaculate, unfailing love of His Father. This unfamiliar perspective, on Earth and far from Heaven, no doubt deepened Jesus' compassion for humanity as He lived alongside them.

Jesus modeled the upside down kingdom in His life on Earth. He most notably shared it with us through the beatitudes recorded in Matthew 5:1-12 and Luke 6:20-26. On their own, they presented what seemed like opposing ideas. They turned the world as people saw it on its head. However, they are swelling with meaning when we read them in the context of what happened before this Sermon on the Mount.

We exit the desert and join Jesus in Luke 6:1-11, where He responds to the accusations of the Pharisees. Jesus and His disciples had plucked harvest from a field, which the Pharisees claimed to be unlawful for the Sabbath (v.2). Jesus responded with an Old Testament account of David that the Pharisees would have memorized. The loaded recollection of 1 Samuel 21:1-9 tells the story of David asking for bread from a priest. The only bread available was the showbread, meant for holy consumption on the Sabbath. David met the specifications of a "clean vessel," and the priest gave him the five loaves (v.6). David consumes the bread without penalty or consequence. On the surface, we can see the contrast between Sabbath rules and human needs.

Jesus did not utter empty words, which we see in these verses. The showbread represented the presence of God. Later in John 6:35, Jesus states that He IS the bread of life. He modeled Communion in Matthew 26:26-30 and asked us to eat the bread, *His body*. Not only was Jesus a clean vessel, but He offered His sacrifice to make us an acceptable offering, as well. He could quote the nuances of Old Testament law with authority because *He was the Law*. Jesus boldly protected the hearts of His people.

Beatitudes

Jesus spent the night before the Sermon on the Mount praying. He awoke to choose His twelve disciples, and together they went to a place where a crowd had gathered for healing. In Luke 6:20-26 (NIV), we read,

> "Looking at his disciples, He said: 'Blessed are you who are poor, for yours is the kingdom of God. Blessed are you who hunger now, for you will be satisfied. Blessed are you who weep now, for you will laugh. Blessed are you when people hate you, when they exclude you and insult you and reject your name as evil, because of the Son of Man. Rejoice in that day and leap for joy, because great is your reward in heaven. For that is how their ancestors treated the prophets. But woe to you who are rich, for you have already received your comfort. Woe to you who are well-fed now, for you will go hungry. Woe to you who laugh now, for you will mourn and weep. Woe to you when everyone speaks well of you, for that is how their ancestors treated the false prophets.'"

Jesus gave meaning to the human experience: the mundane, the profane, and the unbearable. Blessed and broken, He related the two. Jesus said *I see you* to the forgotten and broken. He offered more for what the world called less. Jesus did not admire the rich with full bellies and beautiful homes. Nor did He point to the performative obedience of the Pharisees as an example of living. He shifted the paradigm.

Jesus entered a world filled with rules and laws made to separate, not protect. People were pressed under the thumb of damaging social hierarchies and religious views. Divided by sects and classes, there were apparent ranks—a scarcity of health or wealth isolated people. Jesus came to show this is not how God's kingdom is structured. He sat with sinners and made space for untouchable people. *There was always space at His table.*

First Corinthians 3:18-20 tells us not to rely on the world's wisdom. The Bible warns that it will be foolish compared to God's wisdom. I have felt this increasingly as the world abstracts the facts to make them more palatable. I see the unspoken pain that is renamed and rebranded. We are putting bandaids on bleeding hearts. I have compassion for those who are still searching for answers.

The Gospel calls us to live a life that is upside down to what the world demands. In the following image, you will see a representation of this upside-down kingdom. Two castles suspended in an hourglass mirror each other. The bottom castle represents what we value on Earth, and the upper fortress represents God's kingdom. Earth's highest and most valuable things keep us closest to the horizon.

I imagine our two worlds suspended in an hourglass, measured by time. Drawing closer to the Lord moves us heavenward, creating space between us and this world. The things that will get you the "most" on earth—success, wealth, fame—matter the least in Heaven. The things that matter the most in Heaven are considered lowly here—serving others, sharing in each other's pain, helping out in quiet places, and doing it all with limited praise. The stars in the sky are like sand pouring through the hourglass. Time doesn't matter in Heaven, but here it truly is finite. This hourglass kingdom is a reflection of where we invest our lives. (See Figure 8)

Figure 8
The Upside Down Kingdom

© Out of the Garden

Take it to Heart

- Who are the "Pharisees" in your life? How does this influence the way you think or act?

- Where do you feel the tension of living between two worlds?

Take it to God

- Read the beatitudes in Luke 6:20-26.

- Can you recall a time you felt poor, hungry, mourned, etc.? Take a moment to consider the details.

- How do the beatitudes contrast with what the world says about living in "this condition?"

- What hope do these verses offer you in the face of challenges?

- Pray—express gratitude, disappointment, sadness, joy, etc. Express yourself honestly as you apply the beatitudes to your life.

12

Take this Cup

"Do you believe it is true? That Jesus will save us from the empire?" Judith whispered excitedly into her mother's ear. The windows were open, and you could hear the dull rasp of sheathed swords as armed guards made their rounds. Her younger brother, Jonathan, dipped his fingers in the wet clay and formed tiny daggers.

"He is making an army of men!" He cried out, pretending to jab the air with his weapons. Both women shushed him quickly, and Judith instinctively checked the windows and doorway. Their mother pushed a bowl of pressed grapes and fresh bread in front of the boy and shook her head slowly. She then placed a broken cup on the table and began to work the wet clay into the cracks.

"He did speak of His kingdom here on Earth, but it's not what you think. Remember when the Lord spoke to the prophet Jeremiah? He said, '"Like clay in the hand of the potter, so are you in my hand, Israel. (Jeremiah 18:6, NIV)"' Her clay-stained fingers smoothed the filled edges. "I believe we are to be like this clay. He came to repair *us*, not to destroy *them*. When we are made whole, we are filled with His love, and can be poured out to others." She demonstrated this by taking previously repaired vessels and pouring water from one to the next.

Jonathan held a broken cup above his head and bellowed, "But he could break their cups if he wanted to!" Judith swiped it out of his hands and placed it on the counter; her nose scrunched in quiet annoyance. She silenced him again as she brushed him away from the counter. Their ever-patient mother shook her head and smiled knowingly.

"There are enough broken cups. What a mess it has become, don't you think? Certainly, he could crush the clay and, like the potter, make things new. But look at how beautiful it is to mend and repair what we already have?"

With that, their mother held up a bowl that had suffered several cracks over the years. The repaired clay sprawled up from the bottom like a solidly rooted tree. It filled the broken places with each branch and strengthened what might have otherwise been rendered useless. She arranged pieces of bread in the bowl and motioned her children to sit at the table.

"Broken clay is forgotten,
but mended clay tells the story of second chances."

Jesus came to do abundantly more than conquer Rome.
While this family is fictional, the reality of Roman oppression and Jewish hope fills the pages of history. The people longed to know relief from the Roman Empire. Stories of Moses and the extraordinary rescue out of Egypt made them hopeful for their own miraculous departure. At that time, people lived in scarcity due to financial oppression and physical persecution.

Jesus' own family faced persecution from King Herod. Herod heard a rumor of an infant king and, as a result, had Jewish male infants murdered. Mary and Joseph remained graciously hidden by a humble stable as Jesus entered the world. He was placed in a food trough, already a symbol for the bread of life He would one day become. King Herod thought Jesus threatened *his* kingdom. But Jesus was building a dynasty that would save hearts and begin a legacy. Undistractable, He was focused on a noble cause. He remained faithful to what was set before Him. Interestingly enough, Christianity later contributed to the fall of the Roman Empire. *But I digress.* While Jesus *could* have removed their suffering, He did not allow the temporary to distract Him from achieving the eternal.

Jesus came to interrupt the cycle of sin and separation. A cup represents many things throughout Scripture. A vessel for thanksgiving, comfort, trembling, wrath, blessing upon blessing upon blessing—and so on. The cup is passed through generations, filled with God's wrath, then overflowing with God's love, wrath, mercy, wrath—and so on until Jesus came, took the cup, flipped it, and said, "Do this." In order to be filled, we need to be poured out—emptied of ourselves. He flipped cultural norms on their head.

In the Garden of Gethsemane, Jesus processed the immense weight of the cup (Luke 22:39-44). He no doubt anticipated the physical and emotional pain of being crucified, but more importantly, the separation from His Father. Isaiah 53:5 (NIV) prophesied this when He said, "But He was pierced for our transgressions, He was crushed for our iniquities; the punishment that brought us peace was on Him, and by His wounds we are healed." It was a penalty and a remedy.

Jesus invited His disciples (and us) to remember Him through Communion. Matthew 26:26-29 tells us that He modeled Communion by taking bread, giving thanks, and breaking it to give to His disciples. Jesus introduced Communion as eating His body and drinking His blood, representing the new covenant with Him. He became the final sacrifice, the ultimate price.

Jesus takes our cups, full of our sins and brokenness, and refills them with His love and forgiveness. His blood symbolizes our redemption, our cleansing, and our healing. We drink this regularly to be emptied of ourselves and filled by Him. It's a symbol of what He has done for us and a reminder of the power in that transaction.

Chosen l Blessed l Broken l Given

Henri Nouwen, a Dutch Catholic priest, professor, and writer, spoke on Communion in his sermon, "*Who Are We? Our Christian Identity.*"[28] He noted that Jesus took (or chose), blessed, broke, and gave the elements. Nouwen described us as Communion people, a living Eucharist, a community of believers. He pointed out that just like the elements of the

Eucharist, we are chosen, blessed, broken, and given to the world. We are not left in our brokenness, as God uses it to help others. He does not waste our suffering. Our sins and shortcomings reflect who we are in this world. They point to our experiences, relationships, and the places we've needed grace the most. Our vulnerable places are not meant for others to feast on, which makes the rest He offers that much kinder.

Something beautiful occurred to me as I was listening to Nouwen's sermon. *This rhythm has existed since the beginning of time.* Adam and Eve were chosen by God, blessed in the Garden, broken by sin, and given to the world. The pattern continues with each story of the Bible. Ordinary people are chosen, blessed, and broken for something extraordinary to be given. Each one thumps along with the pulse of a beating heart. *Chosen, blessed, broken, given.* The consistency both deepens my faith and awakens my hope as the cadence lands on given—every time. *It does not end at brokenness.*

As we read the Communion invitation in Matthew 26:26-29, another invitation comes to mind. Earlier, Jesus said, "Come to me, all who labor and are heavy laden, and I will give you rest. Take my yoke upon you, and learn from me, for I am gentle and lowly in heart, and you will find rest for your souls. For my yoke is easy, and my burden is light" (Matt. 11:28-30, ESV).

Come, you are *chosen*.
Take my yoke and learn, be *blessed*.
Find rest for your souls, especially when you are *broken*.
My yoke is easy, and my burden is light.
Let me be your strength as you are *given* to the world.

Communion is an invitation to come before our Savior and be renewed by His sacrifice. It's an opportunity to love the broken cups beside us—cracked, brittle, unclean. The cups that we regularly place before the Lord as we contend with sin. We can rest in knowing that He will bring them back to purpose. We see evidence of this relationship as we face trials with what Philippians 4:7 describes as "peace beyond our understanding." Nouwen stated that "Eucharist is recognition. It is the full realization that the one who takes, blesses, breaks, and gives is the One who, from the beginning of time, has desired to enter into communion with us."[29]

I want you to imagine your life as a cup. God created it with intricate care, Jesus is the healing balm that restores it, and the Holy Spirit acts as a cupbearer, testing what goes into it. Where have you experienced this transformation in your life? Perhaps you cannot shake the sense that you were designed with a purpose. You have undergone restoration from a broken past. That still, small voice that says, *be careful now*, has stirred you to make choices that may have protected you from an unfavorable outcome. Acknowledging where you are today might lead to gratitude, confession, or supplication.

Take your cup—no matter how weathered by time or chipped like a tooth—and place it before Jesus for restoration. Hear the call to be taken and blessed for God's glory. Rest in His loving embrace when you are broken. Listening for the timing to share those pieces with the world. Embrace the abundant life that He has in store for you.

Take it to Heart

- Where do you see the rhythm of Communion in your own life? Chosen, blessed, broken, and given.

- What stage of the cycle are you in now?

- What are some of the ways your brokenness has been given to the world?

Take it to God

- Read Jeremiah 18:1-6. How is God reshaping your life?

- Express gratitude for the ways God has refined your life. Seek His guidance as you face challenges and require rest.

CONCLUSION

The Story Continues

It has been years since Adam and I were banished from the Garden. So much has happened since that painful day. We grow and hunt our food. Break the Earth, plant the seeds, watch it grow, and spread. Break the animal, eat the body, and have strength for the day. My own body has been broken and given. First Cain, then Abel. Some days felt like we were free of the curse. The boys would play, and Adam would smile and touch my arm. It felt like we still knew what the other was thinking. I watched them grow—once tiny beings that kicked my ribs now towered over me.

One nightfall, I twisted my fingers through the lavender buds and sat down beside the river. My belly was swollen as Seth grew inside of me. I mourned for Abel. *How could Cain kill his own brother?* His anger has destroyed our family. My sin has destroyed our family. *Why are we so broken?* Why has God left us here to suffer?

I leaned over the river to wash the tears from my eyes. My reflection was a reminder of how the years have aged me. For a moment, I saw the reflection of my younger self. I instinctively touched my stomach, where I recalled smooth skin and a strong frame. I pulled my clothing tighter when I imagined my former nudity. *I stood tall and was not ashamed to be naked.* I hardly recognized that version of myself.

As I looked in the river, the moonlight bounced off a fish swaying by. I held very still so that it would come back. I was captivated by the way its scales sparkled in the dark water. Seth stirred inside my belly, reminding me I was not alone in the darkness. Something else stirred inside of me, as well. *I recognize this fish from the Garden.* My hand covered my mouth as a gasp escaped me. At this moment, it occurred to me that the water flowing beside me flowed out of my former home. *All is not lost.* He did not destroy the flowers. He did not destroy the rivers. He did not destroy its inhabitants. *He did not destroy us.*

It may sound odd to you today, but I removed my dressing and stepped into the river. The water enveloped my unclothed body. I thanked God for second chances. I praised Him for the small life growing in me, another blessing to ease the pain of losing Abel. I smiled at the memory of our wonderful Garden, and how much more His kingdom would be. That night, under the weight of Adam's arm and serenaded by crickets, I rested in knowing our story wasn't over yet.

ACKNOWLEDGMENTS

I'm not sure where to begin, but there is a small village of people who have cheered me on throughout this process. I've been fortunate to have wise mentors, faithful friends, and a supportive husband. I would like to thank my parents for prioritizing my education over the years and providing examples of hard work. I walked through open doors as a result. To the mentors who walked alongside our marriage and personal ministry—thank you for living it out and cheering us along. For my small team of editors, thank you for taking time out of your busy lives to read these words and offer endless encouragement. Last, but far from least, I'd like to thank my family for your patience throughout this project. To my husband, for being my best friend and loving me through challenges. Thank you for chasing dreams with me. To my kids, for helping me slow down and cherish the moments. I will work very hard to complete the next book while you are all busy at school. I love you dearly and can't wait to see what God has in store for our family.

jen

NOTES

Chapter One
[1] Koleva M, Nacheva A, Boev M. Somatotype, nutrition, and obesity. Rev Environ Health. 2000 Oct-Dec;15(4):389-98. doi: 10.1515/REVEH.2000.15.4.389. PMID: 11199249.
[2] Worchel, S., Lee, J., & Adewole, A. (1975). Effects of supply and demand on ratings of object value. *Journal of Personality and Social Psychology, 32*(5), 906–914.
[3] *Ted Lasso* is a beloved, fictional character played by Jason Sudeikis. The series aired on Apple TV (2020-2023).
[4] Mullainathan, Sendhil and Eldar Shafir, PhD. *Scarcity: The New Science of Having Less and How it Defines Our Lives.* Henry Holt and Co., 2014.
[5] Graeber, David. *Debt: The First 5,000 Years.* Melville House, 2012.

Chapter Two
[6] Of Monsters and Men. *Beneath the Skin* (2015).

Chapter Three
[7] Heshmat, Ph.D., Shahram. *The Scarcity Mindset.* Psychology Today, April 2, 2015.
https://www.psychologytoday.com/us/blog/science-choice/201504/the-scarcity-mindset
[8] *Over the Top (1987)* is a film classic, starring Sylvester Stallone, as he overcomes arm-wrestling foes with a backward hat. Need I say more?

Chapter Four
[9] Whitney, D. Praying the Bible. Crossway, 2015.
[10] Smith, Ph.D., M Cecil. *The Benefits of Writing.* Northern Illinois. University. https://www.niu.edu/language-literacy/_pdf/the-benefits-of-writing.pdf
[11] Armstrong, Michelle. *Encounters at the Feet of Jesus.* The Chapel: Akron. Oct.-Nov. 2020. www.thechapel.life/resources/akron/special-events-classes/encounters-at-the-feet-of-jesus/encounters-at-the-feet-of-jesus-class-1/

[12] Ellison, Davy. *6 Steps for Biblical Word Studies.* The Gospel Coalition, April 11, 2023. www.thegospelcoalition.org/article/six-steps-word-studies/
[13] Mejia, Zameena. *10 Science-Backed Benefits Of Meditation.* Forbes Health, May 3, 2023. www.forbes.com/health/mind/benefits-of-meditation/

Chapter Five

[14] Keith, David. *Backs Against the Wall: The Howard Thurman Story.* Maryland Public Television, 2019.
[15] Pennycook G, Cannon TD, Rand DG. Prior exposure increases perceived accuracy of fake news. J Exp Psychol Gen. 2018 Dec;147(12):1865-1880. doi: 10.1037/xge0000465. Epub 2018 Sep 24. PMID: 30247057; PMCID: PMC6279465.
[16] Lewis, C. S. *The Screwtape Letters.* Geoffrey Bles, 1942.
[17] I'm a huge Swiftie. *There, I said it.* This quote is taken from her song, *Out of the Woods.* Her work is not for all audiences. I appreciate her work and enjoy her take on the human experience.

Chapter Seven

[18] Renaud, Chris, and Kyle Balda. *The Lorax.* Universal Pictures, 2012.
[19] Leaf, Dr. Caroline. *Cleaning Up Your Mental Mess.* Baker Books, 2021.
[20] *Richie's Plank Experience.* Meta Quest, 2021.
[21] The D.A.R.E. Program : a Review of Prevalence, User Satisfaction, and Effectiveness. [Washington, D.C.] :U.S. Dept. of Justice, Office of Justice Programs, National Institute of Justice, 1994.
[22] Ashwood, Professor Ken. *The Brain Book. Firefly Books, 2nd, 2019.*
[23] Carter, Rita, et al. *How the Brain Works.* Penguin Random House, 2020.
[24] Rehman A, Al Khalili Y. Neuroanatomy, Occipital Lobe. [Updated 2022 Jul 25]. In: StatPearls [Internet]. Treasure Island (FL): StatPearls Publishing; 2023 Jan-. Available from: https://www.ncbi.nlm.nih.gov/books/NBK544320/#
[25] MacDonald, James. *Gripped By the Greatness of God.* Moody Publishers, 2005.
[26] McHargue, Mike. *Finding God in the Waves: How I Lost My Faith and Found It Again Through Science.* Convergent Books, 2016.

Chapter Nine

[27] Confucius. The Analects (Lun Yü). Harmondsworth ; New York :Penguin Books, 1979.

Chapter Eleven

[28] Nouwen, Henri. *Who Are We? Our Christian Identity.* https://www.hoopladigital.com/title/11961551
[29] Nouwen, Henri J.M. *With Burning Hearts: A Meditation on the Eucharist Life.* Orbis Books, 2021.

ABOUT THE AUTHOR

Jen Hoffman is a professional counselor with a background in Marriage and Family Therapy. She is trained in the Gottman Method and passionate about helping clients improve relational health. Jen currently works with clients from a diverse background.

Jen is the wife and mom in a party of five. She enjoys time with loved ones, creating, cultivating good things, and moonlighting as an amateur karaoke performer.

In her debut publication, Hoffman combines therapeutic skills with biblical knowledge and just a touch of humor to help others grow in their faith. The goal of this work is to transform lives by sharing the path to a renewed mind.

Made in the USA
Middletown, DE
28 November 2023

43806594R00092